Hobbies

£3·00

40

You Can Play Bridge

PHILLIP ALDER

Cartoons by Robert Donovan

THAMES METHUEN

First published in Great Britain 1983 by
Methuen London Ltd
11 New Fetter Lane, London EC4P 4EE
in association with
Thames Television International Ltd
149 Tottenham Court Road, London W1P 9LL

Reprinted 1984

ISBNs 0 423 00830 7 hardback
0 423 00750 5 paperback

Printed in Great Britain by
Butler & Tanner Ltd, Frome and London

Contents

To Christopher Falkus,
who made me two offers I could not refuse;
Methuens choose their godfathers carefully!

Introduction

I am glad that you have decided to join me for bridge; but although this work is being published in conjunction with the I.T.V. series, it is not feasible for my book to follow the television programmes too closely. Most of the hands that were in the series are in this book, as is, of course, all the bidding theory. But there is quite a lot more as well. I do not want to put you off, but it does take a long time to learn to play bridge well. One can pick up the basics fairly quickly, but one will play very badly. The secret of success is steady application. Read this book at a pace that suits you, find three friends and play as often as you wish, read other bridge literature and try to train your mind to think logically about the game. There are really only two secrets to being a winner at bridge (and though many people will say that they play for fun, they find it much more fun if they win): counting accurately and thinking of the right thing at the right time. I know that that sounds formidable, but you will find it gets easier and easier as you become more familiar with the game. Bridge is the world's greatest card game for four people (poker lays some claim to matching bridge, which is why I have stipulated four players) but as with all of the finer things in life, like wine tasting, it takes time to learn, to gain experience. However, it is worth it in the end.

Bridge, like all walks of life, has its own vocabulary. To take one simple example: consider the word 'ace'; what does it mean to you? To a tennis player it is a serve that the opponent did not even touch with his racquet; to a golfer it is a hole in one, but to a bridge player, of course, it is the top card in any suit, the one with the letter 'A' on it. All the key words have been put in italics, and are included in the glossary at the end of the book.

The chapters have been put into some sort of order, with the bidding first, the card-play and defence second, but you do not have to be like the swimmer who jumps in at the shallow end and swims the whole length under water before surfacing, gasping for breath. You can jump in from different parts of the pool, surface, climb out, and jump in somewhere else. But as each chapter will assume that you have assimilated what has come before, please restrict your leaping to going between the bidding and the card-play.

Each chapter is ended with a quiz so that you can check you have understood the material covered in that section.

All that remains for me to do is to wish you the best of luck; I hope you will give bridge a good try. You never know, maybe one day we will meet at a tournament and you will teach me a thing or two about the game.

1   *The History of Bridge*

I am sorry I have not learned to play at cards. It is
very useful in life: it generates kindness and
consolidates society.

Samuel Johnson

The antecedents of bridge are clouded in uncertainty with different
authorities claiming three or four games that were supposed to be the
ones from which bridge was derived. However, I think it is fair to say
that bridge would not be the game it is today if playing cards had not
been invented, or had not evolved as they have. So let us start there.

It is felt by most researchers that playing cards were invented in
China, 'dotted cards' first appearing in A.D. 1120. These were devised
for the amusement of the Emperor Seun-Ho's various concubines. But
other scholars point out that the Chinese originated paper money in
the seventh century A.D. and, being great gamblers, they would shuffle
this money and invent 'card games'.

Other countries, notably India, Egypt and Italy, have produced their
own packs of cards, but the forefather of our present pack comes from
France. During the fifteenth and sixteenth centuries France became the
chief card-making nation, exporting widely to many European countries.
To a large extent the popularity of the French cards was due to their
simplicity. Each pack had four suits divided into two red and two
black. Being combined with 'pips' they were easy and cheap to produce.
There were 52 cards in each pack divided into four suits, each with an
ace, three coat-cards (now incorrectly known as court-cards) and
numerals two to ten. The coat-cards consisted of a king, a queen and a
valet (a knave or jack). These had names appearing on them, and it is
thought that they represented well-known personages in history,
as follows:

KINGS
Spades: David — pictorially represented as Charles VII of France.

3

David, King of the Jews, obtained his crown after persecu-
tion by Saul, but was troubled by the revolt of his son,
Absalom. Charles VII, disinherited by his mother, Isabel of
Bavaria, reconquered his kingdom, but was later troubled
by the wickedness of his son, Louis XI.

Hearts: Charlemagne, Emperor of the Franks.
Diamonds: Caesar, the Roman General and First Consul.
Clubs: Alexander, the Greek Emperor.

QUEENS
Spades: Pallas, the Goddess of War and Wisdom, who observed
strict celibacy. Perhaps she was used as a tribute to the
Maid of Orleans. If this were so, it must have been after
1421, and probably before the end of Charles VII's reign
in 1461.
Hearts: Judic — representing Isabel of Bulgaria, wife of Charles VI
and mother of Charles VII.
Diamonds: Rachel — representing Agnes Sorel, Mistress of Charles VII
and famed for her beauty.
Clubs: Argine (an anagram of Regina) — representing Mary of
Anjou, wife of Charles VII.

VALETS
Spades: Ogier, a Danish Champion. There was a French Ogier, but
he was not a man of distinction.
Hearts: La Hire, the famous Etienne de Vignolles who, by his
exploits, did so much to sustain the throne of Charles VII.
There is a story that, when the English were holding Paris
and nearly half of France, Charles VII showed La Hire
preparations for an intended ballet, based on the game of
Piquet, which La Hire had invented, and asked for his
opinion. La Hire replied, 'By my faith, Sire, I think it is
impossible to lose a kingdom more gaily.'
Diamonds: Hector le Galard, famous Captain of Charles VII.
Clubs: Lancelot, one of the Paladins of Charlemagne's Court.

Regarding the above, the Encyclopaedia Britannica of 1839 describes
the four French kings thus: 'The names of the four Kings were David,
Alexander, Caesar and Charles . . . and represent the four monarchies of
the Jews, Greeks, Romans and Franks under Charlemagne.'
    The original coat-cards gave full justice to the glory of the dress and

accoutrements of the people depicted. However, around 1880 reversible cards became standard and so the artistic designs were sacrificed for the benefit of the card players.

Bridge was invented by the American Harold Sterling Vanderbilt on 1st November 1925, but there were several games that have features in common with bridge that were being played before that date.

In 1667 Pepys says that card playing was introduced at Court on a Sunday by Catherine of Braganza, the Portuguese wife of Charles II. She was instrumental in making Ombre the fashionable game for nearly one hundred years. Quadrille, a development of Ombre, inspired Dean Swift to write a paper that includes the first reference to a 'dummy' in a card game. These were trick-taking games using a 40-card pack.

A game called Triumph was played in England in the fifteenth century, and the word 'trump' is a corruption of that. A derivative of Triumph was called Ruff and Honours and it involved the words 'trump' and 'ruff', but not with the same meaning as they have in bridge. And at about this time a game called Whist came into being. Edmund Hoyle wrote the first book about Whist in 1742, including information on card-play, and it was a best-seller in several countries.

Hoyle then introduced Long Whist in which each player received thirteen cards, and another step on the road to bridge had been taken.

Perhaps bidding originates from a Russian game called Vint, which was being played around 1880. There were several versions, but the most popular was a trick-taking game similar to whist in which the players had to say how many tricks they would take in the same way as one does in bridge: the numbers went from one to seven and one added the number called to six to get the number of tricks to be taken. The suits were given a hierarchy which was, in ascending order, spades, clubs, diamonds and hearts. No-trumps were permitted and ranked higher than hearts. There was even scoring similar to that used in rubber bridge, but there was no dummy, no doubling, and the points scored went on an escalating scale with the greater the number bid. (For example, one spade scored 70, whereas four spades was worth 400.)

Another game with some similarities to bridge was Biritch, or Russian Whist. In this game the dealer had the option of nominating the trump suit, or no-trumps, but there was no competitive bidding, though doubling and redoubling was allowed; and the declarer's partner put his hand down on the table after the opening lead. It is of course possible that the name Bridge is derived from Biritch.

In 1894 Lord Brougham introduced Bridge Whist to the Portland Club, and then the game became known as Foster's Bridge after a book about the game with that title written by R.F. Foster in 1900. This was in fact a version of Biritch, and it was given added prestige by the fact that King Edward VII played it regularly.

The next major step was taken in Rampur-Baolia, Eastern Bengal, in 1902. Members of the Indian Civil Service started playing their own variety of bridge in which competitive bidding was permitted. Then in about 1905 Auction Bridge was invented and it remained the most popular card game for some 25 years.

In case the reader is unaware, in Auction Bridge there was no premium in bidding to the value of your cards: one spade made with four over-tricks scored the same as five spades bid and made, and one got the game bonus even though it had not been bid. It was Harold Vanderbilt who formulated the rules that have crystallised into Contract Bridge, though he was supposedly given some help by a young woman who insisted on joining a game on board a pleasure cruiser called the *Finland*.

Even though she knew that Vanderbilt and his friends had a regular game, suitably fortified by alcohol she forced her way into the game and then apparently made up new rules as the game was progressing. Afterwards Vanderbilt went back to his cabin and produced a new scoring table that took into account the 'vulnerability' that this anonymous woman had proposed.

If I may be permitted a small commercial, in May 1926 the first issue of *Bridge Magazine* was published, and bridge literature had begun. *Bridge Magazine* is still being published every month to this day, which gives some idea of the way the popularity of bridge has been sustained during the last sixty years or so.

Let us hope that you will soon be adding yourself to the growing list of regular bridge players, not just in Britain but the world over.

Section A

The Bidding

2   *The Basic Elements of the Game*

Digo, paciencia y barajar.
What I say is, patience and shuffle the cards.
                                        Miguel de Cervantes

Bridge is played using a normal pack containing 52 cards – the jokers
are discarded. The 52 cards are divided into four *suits*: clubs (♣),
diamonds (◊), hearts (♡) and spades (♠). The order in each suit is:
ace highest, then king, followed by the queen, the jack (or, as some
people still say, the knave*), the ten, nine, and so on down to the two.

The game is played by four people, who are formed into two *partnerships*, with the partners sitting opposite each other. You can form
partnerships by almost any means that you like, but if you are going to
play a social game of *rubber bridge* at home, the normal way is to
draw cards. Spread one pack across the table, and each draw a card.
The two with the highest cards play against the two with the lowest.
(If two players draw identical cards, the tie is split by considering the
suits of the cards. The order is the reverse to the one given above, for
a reason that will become apparent soon. So the ten of spades is considered a higher card than the ten of hearts – but only when cutting
for partners.)

The four players sit around a square table, which is usually covered
in green baize. For the sake of ease, they are referred to in print by the
four cardinal points, so North plays with South against East and West.

The player who cut the highest card becomes the *dealer* of the first
hand. The person on the dealer's left shuffles the pack before passing
it to his partner, who cuts the cards by moving the top portion towards
the dealer. (It is normal to use two packs of cards, the partner of the
dealer shuffling the second pack in preparation for the following hand.

*In *Great Expectations*, Estelle says of Pip, 'He calls the knaves, Jacks,
this boy.'

11

Usually the packs will have different coloured backs, and the person who drew the highest card can choose which pack he or she would like to deal — superstition is as rife in bridge as in all astrological walks of life.) The dealer lifts the bottom section of the pack, places it on top of the bottom half to reconstitute all 52 cards, and proceeds to *deal*. This is done by going in a clockwise direction, giving one card at a time to each player. Obviously, after thirteen navigations of the table the cards will have been distributed. (This ritual might seem rather particular, but it has to be done one way or another, and this one has stood the test of time.)

Everyone then picks up their cards and sorts them into suits. At this point the first half of the game begins: the *auction*. It is a similar process to that which takes place in Sotheby's or Christies. Each side vies to try to win the auction, which decides the suit that will be trumps, or if there will be no trumps (NT), and how many tricks the winning side in the auction will have to take in order to make their *contract*.

As in an ordinary auction, there is an opening price at which the *bidding* must begin. There will be thirteen *tricks* to be won during the play of the cards as each player must contribute one card to each trick. To win more tricks than your opposition, you must therefore take at least seven. The lowest possible bid is one, so the first six tricks are assumed, and to each bid you must add six to get the number of tricks that need to be won in order to make your contract. Therefore, a bid of one heart means that you think you can make seven tricks with hearts as trumps; a bid of four clubs suggests that you are willing to try to make ten tricks with clubs as trumps (6 + 4 = 10).

In bidding, as in a real auction, each call must be higher than the previous one. This means that the suits must be given an hierarchy, and it is easy to remember because it is alphabetical: the lowest suit is clubs, and then, in ascending order, come diamonds, hearts and spades. No-trumps breaks the rule because it is the highest of all, it being considered more dangerous to try to play the hand without the safety of a trump suit.

In practical terms this means that you can overcall one club with one of any other suit or no-trumps, but if you wish to overcall one diamond with a club bid, you must call two clubs. Given this, what is the highest bid you can make, one that cannot be overcalled?

There are thirteen tricks available, you ignore the first six, so the bid must be seven. The highest rank is given to no-trumps, so the maximum bid is seven no-trumps. It is as if there is a ladder, one club being the lowest rung, then one diamond, one heart, one spade, one no-trump, two clubs, two diamonds, and so on up to seven no-trumps. Each time you make a bid, you must climb at least one rung higher than the previous bidder.

There is no compulsion to bid. If you think your hand does not justify any action, you can say, 'No bid.' (That is in Britain; the rest of the world says, 'Pass.')

The bidding starts with the dealer and progresses in a clockwise direction until there has been a positive bid followed by three 'no bids'. (Of course, it is possible that none of the players wishes to start the bidding, in which case there will be four passes, the cards are thrown in and the other pack dealt by the person to the previous dealer's left.)

So an auction might proceed something like this: East, the dealer, 'One heart.' South, 'Two clubs.' West, 'No bid.' North, 'Three clubs.' East, 'No bid.' South, 'No bid.' West, 'No bid.' As you can see, rather lengthy when written out for such a short bidding sequence. So in bridge books and magazines, a bidding diagram is used, and for that auction it looks like this:

West	North	East	South
		1♡	2♣
No	3♣	No	No
No			

Don't worry that you do not understand why each player did what I have hypothesised; one cannot do the proverbial running before the actual walking.

After the bidding comes the card-play. The partnership that made the highest bid has to try to make the stated number of tricks. In the above example North-South have to make nine tricks with clubs as trumps. The person who made the first bid in the final trump suit (or no-trumps, of course) plays the hand. Using the above example again, it is *South* who plays the contract, not North, even though it was North who made the last positive call in the auction; South had bid clubs first. The person who is to play the hand is called the *declarer*.

The opponent to the declarer's left, West in our example, leads a card; in bridge parlance, he makes the *opening lead*. Then the partner of the declarer, North, puts his hand down on the table for all to see. He becomes the *dummy* (or in France, *le mort*; would you prefer to be a cabbage or a corpse?) and takes no further constructive part in the hand. The declarer plays the cards from both the dummy and his own hand; an obvious advantage because he can see all the assets at his disposal, whereas the defenders must try to visualise their partner's hand. It is traditional for the declarer to call the cards he wants to play from the dummy and for his partner to put them in the middle of the table, though he can reach across and remove them from the other cards still to be played.

Each trick is made up of four cards, one from each player, with their being played in a clockwise direction, just like the bidding. The highest card played in a suit wins the trick, and the person who played that card leads to the next trick. Every player must follow suit if he can, but he can play any card he wishes from that suit; there is no compulsion to try to win a trick. (In fact knowing when to let the opposition win a trick that you could have taken is one of the arts of the game and will be covered in the card-play section.) If one cannot follow suit, one either throws any card from another suit, or one can try to win the trick by playing a card from the trump suit (*trumping*, or *ruffing*, as it is often called). Any trump beats any card from any other suit.

To go back to our example, let us assume that West leads the six of hearts. North plays the five of hearts, East the king of hearts and South the two. East has won the trick and leads to the next one. Let us assume he plays the ace of hearts. South does not have any left and so he plays the two of clubs, a trump as the contract is three clubs. Both West and North play small hearts and South has won the trick. He leads to the next one, and so on until all thirteen have been completed.

These tricks can be shown by using what is called a *hand diagram*. They look like this:

♡ 5

♡ 6
```
+-------+
|   N   |
| W   E |
|   S   |
+-------+
```
♡ K

♡ 2

for the first trick, and:

♡ x

♡ x
```
+-------+
|   N   |
| W   E |
|   S   |
+-------+
```
♡ A

♣ 2

for the second.

It is traditional that an 'x' is used for any small card that has not been specified. You will remember that I said West and North played small hearts.

Of course having one diagram for each trick is very space-consuming, and it is normal to have one diagram for the whole deal, all 52 cards, but at the beginning we will take it slowly.

Scoring

As in virtually all sports, you win by getting a greater number of points than your opponents. You will find that the scoring is not as complicated as it might appear at first sight.

Clubs and diamonds are called the *minor suits*, and hearts and spades are the *majors*. Because one has to bid higher with the majors, they score more points. For each bid in a minor you score 20 points. So two clubs is worth 40, three diamonds 60, and so on. However, the majors are worth 30 points. This means that two spades scores 60, the same as three clubs or diamonds, but you need to make only eight tricks, not nine.

No-trumps rank higher than the majors, so it will come as no surprise to learn that they are worth even more still. The first trick has a value of 40, and all the subsequent ones have a value of 30. So two no-trumps scores 70, three no-trumps 100. (That figure of 100 is an important one, as you will soon find out.)

In rubber bridge one uses a score-sheet that looks like this:

WE	THEY

The line drawn across the middle divides the points scored for the tricks bid and made, which go below the line, from the bonus and penalty points. Suppose you bid to three spades and make ten tricks, one more than the nine you said you would collect. Three spades bid and made scores 90 (3 x 30), and that score goes below the line. But the *overtrick* is also worth 30, and that is written above the line. So the score-sheet now looks like this:

WE	THEY
30	
90	

If the opponents then call two diamonds and make ten tricks, what will the sheet look like?

They get 40 below the line for the bid of two diamonds, which said that they would make eight tricks. The extra two are also worth 40, but they go above the line, giving:

WE	THEY
30	40
90	40

The key value below the line is 100 points. When you get that many, you are said to have made *game*. That wipes the slate clean below the line, which is done by drawing a line across the sheet.

If you have not made a game you are said to be *non-vulnerable*, whereas if you have made a game you are *vulnerable*.

Any contract that, if made, does not score 100 or more points, is called a *partscore*. If the contract does score at least 100, it is called a game contract. Quickly calculate which contracts are partscores and which are games.

As no-trumps count 40 for the first trick and 30 for each subsequent, a bid of three no-trumps, if made, scores 100 points; game. Four clubs is only worth 80, so that and four diamonds are partscores. Four hearts, however, scores 120 and so is a game contract. All contracts above four hearts are worth at least 100.

To continue our hypothetical *rubber* (hence the name rubber bridge), if after your contract of three spades making ten tricks and their of two diamonds, also making ten tricks, let us assume that they then bid two no-trumps and make it exactly. That is worth 70 points below the line, giving them a total of 110. That being more than 100, they have won the first game and the score-sheet looks like this:

WE	THEY
30	40
90	40
	70

What happens if you get really bold and try to make twelve or even all thirteen of the tricks? For such a risky proposition surely you deserve some extra points. Well, the originators of the scoring agreed. A twelve trick contract is called a *small slam* and carries a bonus of 500 when non-vulnerable and 750 when vulnerable.

To try to make all the tricks is said to be attempting to make a *grand slam*. If successful, the partnership gets a bonus of 1000 if non-vulnerable, or 1500 if vulnerable. These points are in addition to the trick points and go above the line.

There is one other bonus you can collect. If you play in a suit contract and in either your hand or the dummy, but *not* the two hands combined, you have four of the top five cards (A, K, Q, J and 10) you score 100 points above the line. If you have all five you get 150 above the line. These cards are called the *honours*, and the bonuses are called *honour points*. If the contract is in no-trumps you score 150 points above the line if either your hand or the dummy, but not the two hands combined, contains all four aces. You get these points irrespective of how many tricks you make in your bid contract.

What happens if you fail to make the number of tricks you said you would? Then you are said to have *gone down,* and the opposition collects penalty points. If you are non-vulnerable (you have not yet made a game), you lose 50 points for each trick you are short of your target. So if you bid four spades and only made eight tricks, the penalty is 100 because you were two tricks short of your ten-trick target.

If you are vulnerable (you have made a game), the penalty becomes 100 per trick you are short. So if you have bid five clubs but only make seven tricks, you are four short of your target and the opposition collects 400 if you are vulnerable. These penalty points go above the line.

There are two other calls I have not mentioned so far. Apart from the limited vocabulary of the seven numbers and the five denominations, one can also say 'double' or 'redouble' if there has been a positive bid. (There is no rung below one club on which double or redouble sits.) What happens if the opposition lands in a contract that you do not think they will make? Do you just have to sit back and collect the penalty points? As if you had not already guessed, the answer is in the negative. You can 'double' them. If they go down, you get more points, but, of course, if they make it anyway, they get extra points.

If they make it, they double the bid trick value and put that below the line. So two clubs doubled and made, instead of 40 points below the line, scores 80. They also collect 50 points above the line 'for the insult'. If the double was so badly judged that they make overtricks,

"SEVEN NO-TRUMPS REDOUBLED —
MUSTN'T FORGET 50 FOR THE INSULT"

they get 100 per overtrick above the line when non-vulnerable, and 200 per overtrick when vulnerable.

Now let us assume you knew what you were doing (it was your partner who doubled when they made the contract) and they go down. If non-vulnerable the first undertrick gives you 100 points, every subsequent one 200. If vulnerable, they pay out 200 for the first undertrick and 300 for each subsequent. So five diamonds doubled, vulnerable and four down gives 1100 to the opposition.

What happens if you double and the opposition feel that you are not going to get them down? They can redouble. If they were wrong and your double was correct, the penalties are just twice those explained above that you collect when it is only doubled, not redoubled, too. So three down redoubled, non-vulnerable is worth 1000.

If your partner doubled, they redoubled and made it, the trick scores are just redoubled and go below the line; and any overtricks are just double the value for doubled overtricks. However the '50 for the insult' stays at 50!

As a quick example, if they play in three hearts redoubled and vulnerable and make eleven tricks, they score 360 below the line (4 x 90) and 850 above the line (2 x 400 + 50 for the insult).

The last facet of the scoring comes up when a rubber is finished. If one pair wins it by two games to nil, they collect a bonus of 700. If it is two games to one the bonus is 500. (And if you have to break up the game with a rubber unfinished, a pair that has scored a game collects 300 points, and there is 50 given for any partscore.)

As that completes the scoring for rubber bridge, we can put it all in a table:

TRICK SCORES — Below the Line

	Undoubled	Doubled	Redoubled
For each trick bid and made			
in ♣ or ♦	20	40	80
in ♡ or ♠	30	60	120
in No-Trumps — the first trick	40	80	160
— every subsequent trick	30	60	120

GAME is 100 points below the line

PREMIUM & PENALTY POINTS — Above the Line

	Non-vulnerable			Vulnerable		
PREMIUMS	Undoubled	Doubled	Redoubled	Undoubled	Doubled	Redoubled
Each Overtrick	Trick value	100	200	Trick value	200	400
Slam Bonuses Small	500	500	500	1000	1000	1000
Grand	750	750	750	1500	1500	1500
For making a Doubled or Re-doubled Contract	—	50	50	—	50	50
PENALTIES						
1 undertrick	50	100	200	100	200	400
2 undertricks	100	300	600	200	500	1000
3 undertricks	150	500	1000	300	800	1600
4 undertricks	200	700	1400	400	1100	2200
5 undertricks	250	900	1800	500	1400	2800
6 undertricks	300	1100	2200	600	1700	3400
7 undertricks	350	1300	2600	700	2000	4000

Rubber Bonus Scores
Two Game Rubber — 700
Three Game Rubber — 500
One Game in an Unfinished Rubber — 300
Partscore(s) in an Unfinished Rubber — 50

Honour Points — Must all be in the Same Hand

Suit Contract: 4 of top 5 — 100
All 5 — 150

No-Trump Contract: 4 Aces — 150

Now have a go at the quizzes to check that you have got the ideas, but do not be too bothered if the mathematics are somewhat cumbersome; the other players will help out, or you can refer to the table until it becomes almost second nature, which it will in time however poor you consider yourself to be at arithmetic.

QUIZ

1. How many tricks must you make to fulfil the following contracts?
a. Three spades b. Six hearts c. Four diamonds d. Three no-trumps.
2. Which of these auctions could actually take place? If you think one is illegal, explain why.

a.
West	North	East	South
1♡	No	2♣	No
3♣	No	5♣	No
No	No		

b.
West	North	East	South
1◇	No	1♣	No
2♣	No	No	No

c.
West	North	East	South
No	No	No	No

d.
West	North	East	South
2♠	No	No	

e.
West	North	East	South
No	1◇	No	2♠
No	4♠	No	No
No			

f.
West	North	East	South
		No	1♡
1NT	2♡	2◇	No
No	No		

3. What is the greatest number of consecutive partscore contracts you can play before scoring game below the line?
4. What are the scores, stipulating what goes above the line and what goes below, for the following contracts? I am assuming there are no points for honours.

a. Two hearts bid and made exactly.
b. Three clubs made with an overtrick.
c. Four hearts one down non-vulnerable.
d. Two no-trumps made with two overtricks.

e. Six clubs bid and made non-vulnerable.

f. Two clubs doubled, down four non-vulnerable.

g. Two spades doubled and made with two overtricks, vulnerable.

h. Seven spades redoubled and down one, vulnerable.

i. Five clubs doubled and made exactly, non-vulnerable.

j. Three no-trumps redoubled and made with four overtricks, vulnerable.

5. What is the biggest penalty you can concede? What would the contract be?

Answers on page 184

3 *Starting the Bidding*

Ramp up my genius, be not retrograde;
But boldly nominate a spade a spade.

Ben Jonson

Now we get down to the actual bidding, deciding when to bid and what to bid. The idea in the bidding is to tell your partner how strong your hand is and which long suits you have. At the same time he is doing the same thing, so you can add your combined values together and get some idea of how high to bid. Also you are looking for a *suit fit*, a suit in which you have a combined holding of at least eight cards. If you cannot find one then it is usual that you will play the hand in no-trumps. Why eight cards? To give you a reasonable majority, to use Parliamentary terminology. If you have only seven trumps in your two hands, the opposition has six: a majority of only one; clearly not enough to run a government. But if you have eight trumps, they have only five, giving you a workable majority of three. Of course, if you have even more trumps between you, so much the better. But an eight-card fit is considered the acceptable minimum with which to run a bridge hand.

When you pick up your thirteen cards you will check how many honours you have. Clearly the more you have, the better, as honours usually take tricks, whereas low cards have a worse batting average.

Let us consider four different tricks in no-trumps. An ace will win a trick every time.

The king will win three tricks out of four, depending on who holds the ace. These are the possibilities:

a. Ax
Kx

b.
Ax
Kx

c.
AK

d.
Ax
Kx

South's king is in danger only when West has the ace. West will keep his ace until South plays that king, then he will take the trick with his ace. But if East has the ace, declarer can lead a small card from North and what can East do? If he plays the ace, South plays a small card, keeping his king for later; and if East plays a small card, South can play his king and win the trick.

The queen and jack together are approximately equivalent to the king, so it seems reasonable to count an ace as worth four points, a king three, a queen two and a jack one. This scheme of counting points in order to evaluate a hand was invented by Milton Work; they are called *high-card points*.

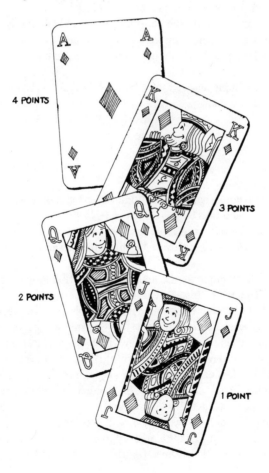

How many high-card points do the following hands have?

a. ♠ A Q 6 5   b. ♠ 10 8 7   c. ♠ A K Q J
    ♡ K J 3   ♡ A Q 4   ♡ A K Q
    ◇ 8 6 5   ◇ K Q J 7 5 4   ◇ A K Q
    ♣ 9 7 6   ♣ A   ♣ A K Q

The first one has one ace (4), one king (3), one queen (2) and one jack (1), giving a total of ten points. As there are ten points in each suit, there is a total of 40 in the pack. As these are divided amongst the four players, the average expectancy is ten points.

The second hand has sixteen points, two aces worth eight plus three for a king, four for two queens and one for a jack.

The third hand you will see about twice a week! Obviously, it is the greatest number of points you can hold; you have every honour card except three jacks, each worth one point. So subtract three from 40 and you get 37.

That seems simple enough, but life is always tougher in reality. Compare these two hands:

d. ♠ A K Q J   e. ♠ A K Q J 10 9 8 7 6 5 4 3 2
    ♡ 4 3 2   ♡ None
    ◇ 4 3 2   ◇ None
    ♣ 4 3 2   ♣ None

With spades as trumps, ignoring the dummy for the moment, how many tricks will each hand take?

Clearly the first will take four, the top trumps, whereas the second cannot fail to collect all thirteen. Yet both have exactly ten high-card points.

This extreme example should make it obvious that long suits tend to be an asset. There are thirteen cards in every suit. If you have four, there are nine to be divided amongst the other players. On average they will have three each, and then your fourth card will be the last one left after three rounds of the suit have been played. But quite often another player will have four cards as well (if not more than four) and you will find life less easy. But as soon as you have five cards in a suit, things improve. There are eight to be divided out among the other players, and each will get $2\frac{2}{3}$ on average; but, of course, one cannot get a fraction of a card. So two players will get three and the third only two; or one will get four and the others two each; and so on through all the possibilities. Most of the time after three rounds of the suit, the last two remaining will be in your hand, and if it is a no-trump contract, you can cash them and the opposition can do nothing about it. If it is the trump suit, you will be able to use the last two to trump winners that the opposition are trying to run when you are out of a suit.

To try to allow for the value of long suits, it is normal to add one point for every card over four that you have in a suit. So a five-card suit is worth one bonus point, a six-card suit two points, and so on. These are called *distributional points*.

How many points do the following hands have, counting both the high-card and distributional points?

f. ♠ A Q 10 9 7	g. ♠ 3 2	h. ♠ K Q J 10 8 7
♡ 6 5	♡ K Q J 10	♡ K Q J 10 8 7
◇ 4	◇ A Q J 6 5	◇ 5
♣ K Q J 7 6	♣ 6 4	♣ None

The first has twelve high-card points and two distributional points, one for the fifth spade and one for the fifth club; a total of fourteen.

The second has thirteen high-card points and one distributional point, also fourteen.

The third has twelve high-card points and four distributional points, a total of sixteen.

The normal requirement to start the bidding at the one level is *thirteen* points, and perhaps only twelve. In the system that is most commonly used in England, the *Acol* system (which was so-named because it was invented in a bridge club in Acol Road, London), *one bids one's longest suit first and next longest suit second as long as each suit contains at least four cards.*

If holding the following hand ♠ A Q 5 4 ♡ K 7 6 ◇ 4 ♣ K Q 10 7 6, having fifteen total points, one would open one club and later bid spades.

This is a simplistic approach, but gives you the general idea. It is also important to realise that, in principle, it is length that is more important than strength. So if holding ♠ 10 8 7 6 5 ♡ A K Q 10 ◇ A K ♣ 10 7 it is correct to open one spade, the longest suit, not one heart, the strongest.

Biddable Suits

I have just mentioned that you need at least four cards to bid a suit, but that is a slightly simplified way of looking at things. If possible one would avoid bidding a four-card suit that was weaker than Q 10 x x, a suit with at least two honours if only headed by the queen. (If the top card is the king or ace it is what we call a biddable suit.)

I can imagine you are wondering what you do when you only have a weak four-card suit worse than Q 10 x x and no other four-card suit. In that unusual circumstance it is permitted to open in a strong three-card minor and then rebid in no-trumps.

In bridge one can never say 'always', and you will have to exhibit some flexibility from time to time, but if you follow these rules, you will not go far wrong.

Balanced Hands

Having seen the basic idea, let us look at particular examples more closely. Apart from the high cards in one's hand, the distribution is important too. One can refer to a hand by stating its distribution. Players will say, 'I held a 5-4-3-1,' meaning that they had five cards in one suit, four in another, three in the third and only one (a *singleton*) in the fourth. It is also possible to refer to the specific suits. If you have 4-0-5-4 shape, you have four spades, no hearts (a *void*), five diamonds and four clubs.

Hands with no singletons or voids and at most one *doubleton* (two cards in a suit) are called *balanced hands*. What distributions can they have?

In order of frequency, the answer is 4-4-3-2 or 4-3-3-3 or 5-3-2-2.

— BALANCED HANDS —

If you hold either of the last two, unless the hand qualifies for a one no-trump opening bid (see the next chapter), bid the one long suit and then rebid in no-trumps to show a balanced hand. (Exactly how this is done will be explained in the next chapter.)

When holding two four-card suits it is slightly more complicated. In my opinion the easiest style is to open the lower-ranking four-card suit. This leaves open the greatest amount of bidding space and allows partner to show his suits easily, leaving you to see if he can bid your other four-card suit. So holding ♠ A Q 10 8 ♡ A Q ◇ A 7 6 ♣ K 5 4 3, open one club.

In my opinion it is correct to tell your partner your *hand type*, whether it is balanced or not, as quickly as possible, and balanced hands suggest that the contract should be played in no-trumps, so bid no-trumps as soon as possible. Obviously if you do find an eight-card fit, then play in that suit if it is a major, as explained at the beginning of the chapter, but otherwise get in those no-trumps.

Unbalanced Hands

An unbalanced hand is any one that is not balanced! It will usually contain a singleton or a void, but it could be 5-4-2-2 or 6-3-2-2, or even 7-2-2-2.

With unbalanced hands, bid your long suits when you have at least four cards in them. If you bid a suit once it shows at least four cards in that suit; if you bid it twice it shows at least five cards; but having said that, a good player will not open with one of a five-card suit and then rebid that suit on the next round if he can avoid it.

If one opens in a suit and then rebids in a new suit it shows at least five cards in the first-bid suit and four (occasionally more) in the second.

If one holds two five-card suits, open one club with both black suits, otherwise start with the higher-ranking. Why is this? When bidding it is preferable to be as economical as possible. To open one club and rebid one heart over a one diamond response is as economical as possible; to open one spade and rebid three diamonds over a two heart response is as uneconomical as possible. If one can save bidding space one does if the bidding is accurate; hence the opening bid being made in the lower-ranking four-card suit when holding two of them. But with five-card suits one is able to rebid them, and when holding two five-carders one has to open in one of the suits and then bid the other one twice to show the distribution of the hand. (To bid a suit once only shows four cards in it; to bid one suit and then another on the second round shows five in the first and four in the second; to bid the second suit again on the third round shows at least five cards in both suits.) Bidding space is saved by opening the higher-ranking of two five-card suits. Suppose you hold both red suits. You open one heart and rebid two diamonds on the next round, hoping to be able to essay three diamonds on the third round to show the shape. However, suppose you were to open one diamond. On the second and third rounds you would have to bid two hearts and three hearts. First of all you are one level higher up the ladder (three hearts rather than three diamonds). And if partner prefers your first suit he must bid four diamonds, whereas if you open one heart he can give preference to hearts at the three level. But when you hold spades and clubs the position is different. To open one club and rebid one spade and then two spades is as economical as possible. Compare that with opening one spade, over which you might have to rebid three clubs and four clubs. So open the higher-ranking of two five-card suits unless they are spades and clubs, when one opens one club.

Holding six-four distribution one has two alternatives: either bid the six-card suit twice and then show the four-card suit if given the chance, or, if the four-card suit is relatively strong, bid it as a five-four initially by opening in the six-card suit and rebidding in the four-carder.

If you have only one six-card suit and no other four-card or longer suit, you can bid it three times. (Once shows four, twice promises five and thrice indicates six.)

Bidding Levels

Because of the bonuses given for bidding and making games and slams, one tries to bid them if one can. To make three no-trumps or four hearts or spades normally needs a combined strength of at least 26 points; but to make five clubs or diamonds usually requires 29 points. This is why priority is given to trying to uncover a four-four major-suit fit. Failing that one considers the feasibility of three no-trumps, only heading to five of a minor if that appears unsuitable, a good fit is present and full values exist.

While I am here I must mention that it usually takes 33 points to make a small slam, and 37 points for a grand.

Combined Point-Count	*Likely Contract Level*
Less than 26	Partscore
26 to 28	3NT, 4♡ or 4♠
29 to 32	Any Game
33 to 36	A Small Slam
37 to 40	A Grand Slam

QUIZ

1. How many points do each of these hands contain?

a. ♠ A J 10 7 6	b. ♠ K 10 7 6 5 4	c. ♠ A Q 10	d. ♠ None
♡ K Q 7 6	♡ 8 7 5 4 3	♡ K J 9 4	♡ A K J 10
◇ K 6	◇ 10	◇ A J 8	◇ A K J 10
♣ A J	♣ 9	♣ K 8 7	♣ Q 5 4 3 2

2. What would be your opening bid with the four hands given above and the four here?

e. ♠ A K Q J	f. ♠ K Q J	g. ♠ K J 9 8 6	h. ♠ K J 9 8 6
♡ A Q	♡ A K J	♡ A 6	♡ A 6
◇ 5	◇ K J 10	◇ Q 10 6 5 3	◇ A
♣ 8 6 5 4 3 2	♣ 10 7 6 3	♣ A	♣ Q 10 6 5 3

Answers on page 185

4   *The Opening Bid of One No-Trump*

With spots quadrangular of di'mond form,
Ensanguin'd hearts, clubs typical of strife,
And spades, the emblem of untimely graves.

William Cowper

When holding a balanced hand, either 4-4-3-2 or 4-3-3-3 or 5-3-3-2 with a five-card minor, it is normal to open one no-trump if your point-count falls within an agreed range. In England it is traditional to play a *weak no-trump*, showing 12-14 high-card points, when non-vulnerable, and a *strong no-trump*, showing either 15-17 or 16-18 high-card points (I prefer the former), when vulnerable. As soon as your hand satisfies the requirements, open one no-trump.

If holding ♠ K J 10 8 ♡ 9 7 5 ◇ A Q 2 ♣ K 7 6 non-vulnerable, open one no-trump. If vulnerable with
♠ A Q 6 ♡ K 5 ◇ K 7 6 ♣ K J 8 4 3, open one no-trump.

What happens when your balanced hand does not have the correct number of points? For the moment, let us assume we are non-vulnerable. With 12-14 points, open one no-trump. With 15 or 16 points, open one of a suit and rebid one no-trump over partner's first bid (which we will come to soon). When holding 17-18 points, open one of a suit and make a *jump rebid* in no-trumps. (A jump bid occurs when you bid at least one level higher than is necessary. If the previous bid was one heart, it is legal to bid one spade, so a bid of *two* spades is a jump.) With 19 points, open one of a suit and rebid three no-trumps.

For example, consider these three hands.

a. ♠ K J 10 8	b. ♠ A Q 6	c. ♠ K J 7
♡ 9 7 5	♡ K 5	♡ A J 4
◇ A Q 2	◇ K 7 6	◇ K Q 9 8 5
♣ K 7 6	♣ K J 8 4 3	♣ K 8

When non-vulnerable, open one no-trump with hand *a* but open one club and rebid one no-trump with hand *b*. Open one diamond with hand *c*; if partner bids one heart, rebid two no-trumps. (If hand *c* had one more point, you would rebid three no-trumps.)

What happens if partner bids two clubs after you have opened one diamond on hand *c*? You must make a jump rebid, so you call three no-trumps. If you have nineteen points, you make the same three no-trump rebid, so partner will only know that you have 17-19 points; the standard trouble with bridge — one can never say 'always'.

If you are vulnerable, what do you do when not in the 15-17 range which opens one no-trump? I am sure you can work it out for yourself. With 12-14 you open one of a suit and rebid one no-trump. With 18 or 19 you open one no-trump and make a jump rebid in no-trumps. However, there is one fly in the ointment. If partner responds at the two level in a suit below the one you have opened (for example, you have opened one heart and he has bid two clubs or two diamonds), a rebid of two no-trumps shows 15-17 points and implies that you have a five-card major or six-card minor (if you have opened one diamond and he has bid two clubs). So you must be careful when you hold 12-14 points to make sure that a response at the two level will not leave you inconvenienced. If you have 5-3-3-2 shape you are all right because you can rebid your five-card suit. But if you are 4-3-3-3 with four hearts or spades, it is correct not to open that suit but one club (or diamond with three small clubs). This is called the *prepared club* because it leaves you able to rebid one no-trump. (Personally I am not keen on this style of bidding, preferring to have four clubs when I open one club, so I use the weak no-trump whatever the vulnerability. However, if your partner has no points, it is possible that the opposition will collect a large penalty by doubling you. So you must recognise the danger attached to opening a weak no-trump when vulnerable. Until you are more experienced I suggest that you play the *variable no-trump*, weak when non-vulnerable, strong when vulnerable.)

Let us have a look at some examples.

d. ♠ K Q 4   e. ♠ A Q 6 4 2   f. ♠ 10 9 6 4
   ♡ A J 8 6   ♡ 10 9 6   ♡ A Q J 8
   ◇ 10 8 6   ◇ A Q J   ◇ A K
   ♣ K 8 7   ♣ K 8   ♣ Q 7 4

When non-vulnerable open *d* with a weak no-trump, but when vulnerable begin with one club. If you open one heart you will be all right if partner bids one spade, but what if he bids two clubs? To rebid two no-trumps would show 15-17 points, so you would be up a creek without a paddle. The answer is to open one club. Then you can rebid one no-trump over one diamond* or one spade. (If partner bids one heart then you can raise to two hearts to show four, but we will cover that in a later chapter.)

On hand *e*, open one spade regardless of the vulnerability. You must show your five-card major. If partner bids at the two level in a new suit, you can rebid two no-trumps to show 15-16 points when non-vulnerable, 15-17 when vulnerable.

With hand *f*, open one heart if non-vulnerable, the lower of two four-card suits, and then rebid two no-trumps over two clubs or two diamonds. If vulnerable, open a strong no-trump.

RESPONSES TO ONE NO-TRUMP

Your partner has opened one no-trump; how do you continue the auction assuming that the next person has passed? You will have an excellent idea of the total number of high-card points that you and your partner hold. Suppose you have ten points. If he has opened a weak no-trump, your total is 22-24, not quite enough for game, so settle in a partscore. But if he has bid a strong no-trump you have 25-27 points, almost certainly enough for game. This is the first evaluation to make.

Second you should judge whether it is better to play in a suit or in no-trumps. It might also be that you need to ask partner to express

---

*Some authors advocate rebidding one heart after one club–one diamond on this hand, but I think it is wrong. It is imperative in my view to show one's hand *type* as soon as possible. This hand is a balanced 12-14 points and should be shown as such, either by opening a weak no-trump or, as in this position, by rebidding one no-trump after the prepared club opener. I like to play that if you open one club and rebid one heart you have virtually guaranteed four hearts and at least five clubs.

an opinion.

Let us look at the different possibilities.

Two Diamonds, Two Hearts or Two Spades

These bids are called *weakness take-outs* and tell partner that you think this contract is safer than one no-trump; he must pass.

You make these bids whenever you hold a five-card or longer suit and do not have enough points to consider looking for game.

There are two important points to make. The bid of, say, two hearts can be made with a very weak hand. Suppose you hold ♠ 6 4 2 ♡ 8 6 5 4 3 2 ◇ 5 3 ♣ 5 3. If partner opens one no-trump, whether it be weak or strong, how much chance do you think he has of making it? Very little, of course. But in two hearts at least you can use your small trumps to ruff any of the other three suits when you are void of them. Because you could hold a hand as weak as this, it explains why the opener must pass.

Second, a weakness take-out might in fact hide a hand with fair values. If you picked up ♠ K J 9 7 6 ♡ 5 3 ◇ A 6 5 ♣ J 8 5 it would be correct to bid two spades opposite a weak no-trump. Your partner might make one no-trump with the help of your nine points and five-card spade suit, but analyses have shown that the odds favour bidding two spades with this hand. Most of the time two spades will be a better contract than one no-trump.

You are also probably asking yourself what happens if you have clubs. No, I have not forgotten that suit, but I am leaving a bid of two clubs to last, for a reason that will be apparent when you read the relevant section.

Two No-Trumps

If partner opens a weak no-trump and you hold twelve points and a balanced hand, you know that your combined assets are 24 to 26 points. The top range is enough for three no-trumps, the bottom level is not. So you raise to two no-trumps, which asks partner to go on to three no-trumps if he has a maximum one no-trump opener. What is a maximum? Well, any fourteen points, or a 'good' thirteen. By 'good' I mean a hand with useful intermediate cards, the tens, nines and eights. Compare these two thirteen pointers:

♠ K Q 10 8	♠ K Q 5 2
♡ A 10 9	♡ A 4 3
◇ K J 9 8	◇ K J 4 3
♣ 10 8	♣ 5 2

Doesn't the first hand look stronger? All those high spot cards are more likely to be worth tricks than the fives, fours, threes and twos, particularly as you will be playing in no-trumps.

Three Clubs, Three Diamonds, Three Hearts or Three Spades

These bids all show at least five-card suits and are *forcing to game*. In other words, the responder has enough values to think that he can guarantee a game contract, and the opener must not pass until at least game has been reached.

If the bid was three of a major (spades or hearts, remember), opener looks to see how many of that suit he has. If he only holds two he cannot be sure of the magic eight-card fit, so he bids three no-trumps. However, with three or four cards the opener can guarantee at least an eight-card fit, so he raises to game: four spades or four hearts.

If the responder has bid three clubs or three diamonds things are not so simple. As five clubs or five diamonds means that one needs to win eleven tricks, one only heads off in that direction with values to spare. So the normal procedure is that the opener bids three no-trumps with only a doubleton in the bid minor, or shows suits that contain *stoppers* (card combinations that will normally win at least one trick) below the level of three no-trumps.

Consider these hands after a one no-trump opener and a three club response.

g. ♠ A Q 6	h. ♠ A Q 6	i. ♠ A Q 6
♡ K J 10 6	♡ K J 10 6	♡ K J 10 6
◇ Q J 7 6	◇ 6 5 3	◇ Q J 9
♣ 6 4	♣ K 8 7	♣ 10 8 6

With *g* you bid three no-trumps because you have only a doubleton club. On *h* you bid three hearts, showing at least three clubs and denying a diamond stopper. (Suppose partner holds a singleton small diamond; the opposition will probably be able to cash at least five diamond tricks to defeat three no-trumps, but you should be able to make five, or six, clubs. However, if partner holds a diamond stopper or two, he can bid three no-trumps himself.) Finally, holding hand *i* you should bid three no-trumps. Even though you hold three clubs, they are small ones and you have stoppers in all the other suits. This is bidding by using one's brain rather than by rigidly applying rules.

— TWO-LEVEL RESPONSE: WEAK; THREE-LEVEL: STRONG —

Three No-Trumps

This is a value bid, telling partner that you think he can make three no-trumps, game in no-trumps. Opposite a weak no-trump it normally shows a balanced hand with no interest in a suit contract and at least thirteen high-card points. However, if you have a strong minor suit you might bid three no-trumps with less points. Suppose you hold ♠ A 6 ♡ 10 9 8 ◇ 10 8 ♣ K Q J 10 8 7. If partner has the ace of clubs he can cash six club tricks and your ace of spades. With at least another eight points in his hand he must surely be able to make two more tricks for the nine that you need. If partner does not have the ace of clubs, he will be able to lead a club, wait for them to take their ace and then re-enter your hand with the ace of spades to run the clubs. Again he must have a good chance of making three no-trumps. The bonus that one receives for making a game justifies taking a slight risk from time to time if you think there is a reasonable chance of collecting the required number of tricks.

Four Hearts and Four Spades
You make these bids when you think that you want to play in these
contracts. For example, suppose you pick up
♠ A Q 10 8 7 6 5 ♡ K 4 ◇ K 4 ♣ 5 4 and partner opens a weak
no-trump. What contract would you like to play in? You know that
you have at least nine spades between you, and that the total points
are 27-29, counting your distributional and high-card points. That is
enough for game, and the spade fit dictates that you bid four spades,
confident that you will make it.

Four No-Trumps
Suppose that partner has opened a weak no-trump and you have a
balanced hand with nineteen points. Your combined strength is 31-33
points, and so you want to play in six no-trumps if partner has a maximum, but not if he has a minimum. Therefore, like the raise to two
no-trumps considered above, you bid four no-trumps, which asks
partner to pass with a minimum, but go on to a slam with a maximum.

Two Clubs
Now we come to the first bid that you will have met that is not used in
its natural sense. So far every time a suit has been bid, you have had at
least four cards in that suit (if we ignore the uncommon 'prepared
club'). However, occasionally you will find that you cannot learn what
you need to know by natural means; you have to resort to what is
called a *conventional bid*, one that has an artificial meaning that you
have already agreed with your partner (and have to tell the opponents
about as well).

Suppose you hold the following hand:
♠ A Q 6 4 ♡ K Q 9 5 ◇ 5 3 ♣ A 6 5 and your partner opens with a
weak no-trump. What do you bid? You have a balanced hand and
enough points for game, so I guess that you would bid three no-trumps
given what I have been through so far. But I have also said that one
plays in four of a major rather than three no-trumps if one can locate
an eight-card fit. Partner might have opened one no-trump holding
♠ K J 10 7 ♡ A J 3 ◇ 7 6 ♣ K J 10 8. If you play these combined
hands in three no-trumps and the opposition leads diamonds, you will
be very lucky to make it; whereas if you play in spades you will make
ten tricks most of the time and eleven occasionally. However, having
said that, partner might have opened one no-trump with
♠ K J 7 ♡ J 10 4 ◇ K Q 10 9 4 ♣ K 8. Now three no-trumps is the

perfect contract, making nine or more tricks depending on how the play goes.

How do you know which hand partner holds? The answer to this problem was solved independently by two people: Jack Marx in England, who was one of the inventors of the Acol system, and Sam Stayman in the United States. Perhaps because he made it more well-known, Stayman's name has been attached to the gadget. *A bid of two clubs over partner's one no-trump opening bid asks him if he has any four-card majors.* This is called the *Stayman Convention.*

— STAYMAN —

Partner responds as follows:

2◇: Sorry partner, I do not have a four-card major

2♡: I have four hearts, and I might have four spades as well

2♠: I have four spades, but I do not have four hearts.

This easily solves your problem when you hold

♠ A Q 6 4 ♡ K Q 9 5 ◇ 5 3 ♣ A 6 5; you bid two clubs, Stayman. If the opener responds two diamonds, you bid three no-trumps, confident that the diamond suit should be safe as he holds at least seven minor-suit cards. However, if he bids two hearts or two spades, you raise to game: four hearts or four spades.

That is the Stayman Convention in its simplest form, but as with most things in life, it has other uses too.

You can use Stayman on very weak hands. Imagine that you pick

up ♠ 5 4 3 2 ♡ 5 4 3 2 ◇ 6 5 4 3 2 ♣ None, my average hand when
playing for money! If partner opens one no-trump and the next person
passes, which contract would you like to play in? Yes, it all depends
on partner's hand. The answer is to bid two clubs, Stayman. If he bids
two hearts or two spades you know you have an eight-card fit and can
happily pass. If, on the other hand, he bids two diamonds you must
also pass. Most of the time it will be an eight- or nine-card fit. Only if
partner has exactly 3-3-2-5 shape will it be only a seven-card fit, but it
will still be better than playing in one no-trump, when your hand would
be totally useless, because he can make some tricks by ruffing clubs
in your hand.

Let me change your hand slightly to
♠ 6 5 4 3 2 ♡ 6 5 4 3 2 ◇ 3 2 ♣ 2, another collection I know well!
What do you bid after your partner has opened one no-trump, weak
or strong? You would like to play in the better major-suit fit, so bid
two clubs. If your partner bids two hearts or two spades, pass con-
tentedly in the knowledge of a nine-card fit. But what happens if he
bids two diamonds? Then the correct thing to do is to bid two hearts.
This tells partner that you have a weak hand with both majors. If he
has three hearts he should pass, but if he has two hearts and three
spades, he should convert to two spades.

Next: ♠ 6 5 4 3 2 ♡ 5 4 3 2 ◇ 3 2 ♣ 3 2. (Won't it be great
actually to start playing and see some honour cards for a change!)
Partner opens one no-trump and you bid two clubs. If he says two
hearts or two spades, pass; but if he rebids two diamonds, bid two
spades. It will be either a five-two or five-three fit, and it will assuredly
be better than one no-trump. (When you make this bid partner will
know you wish to play in two spades but that you have four hearts as
well as five spades.)

There is one other weak hand that uses Stayman: one that wishes
to make a weakness take-out into clubs. You bid two clubs and over the
response, rebid three clubs, which tells partner to pass. Obviously it
is slightly worse to have to play at the three level rather than the two
level, but just think of all the other uses Stayman can be put to which
would not be possible if two clubs were also a weakness take-out. It
is a small price to pay.

That covers the weak hands that can use Stayman. Now we proceed
onto the better ones. Assume that partner has opened a weak no-trump
and you hold ♠ K J 10 7 6 ♡ A 8 6 ◇ K 7 5 ♣ 4 2, twelve points
including distribution. Your combined assets are 24-26, so if partner

has a maximum you would like to play in game, either three no-trumps if he has a doubleton spade, or four spades if he has three or four spades. You cannot respond an immediate two spades because he will pass; and if you bid an immediate three spades it is forcing to game regardless of your partner's hand. So you respond two clubs, and over two diamonds or two hearts by your partner, you rebid three spades. This bid is invitational − it is inviting partner to go on to game if he has a maximum. (If partner in fact responds two spades to Stayman, I think you should bid four spades, not three. The nine-card fit is worth an extra point or two.) If he was a minimum, though he passes three spades.

If you have a hand similar to this one but with five clubs or diamonds, just raise to two no-trumps. Even if partner has a maximum, you will never make five of your minor, for which you normally need 29 combined points. You have to hope that your minor-suit will produce some tricks in no-trumps.

The last problem concerns a hand like this one:

♠ A Q 9 7 ♡ K 6 ◇ K Q J 7 ♣ 8 6 2. Your partner opens a weak no-trump, you respond two clubs looking for the possible spade fit and he bids two hearts. This means that he has four hearts, but he might have four spades too; how do you find out? The answer is that you jump to three no-trumps. Partner will ask himself why you bid three no-trumps after using Stayman rather than just bidding three no-trumps on the first round. To use Stayman you must have been interested in a major-suit fit. He has shown hearts and you have not supported, so he knows that you must have four spades. If he has four spades as well, he should correct to four spades.

The same thing happens if you make the responding hand only worth an invitational sequence: ♠ A Q 9 7 ♡ K 6 ◇ Q J 5 4 ♣ 8 6 2. You bid two clubs looking for the major-suit fit. If partner bids two spades, you raise to three spades, asking partner to bid four spades with a maximum. If instead he responds two diamonds denying a major, you bid two no-trumps, again asking partner to raise to three no-trumps with a maximum. However, what happens if he bids two hearts? He might or might not have four spades. The answer is similar to the last sequence: you bid two no-trumps and partner will know you have four spades. If he has a minimum no-trump without four spades he will pass. If he has a minimum with four spades he will bid three spades and you should pass. If he has a maximum without four spades he will raise to three no-trumps, and, finally, if he has a maximum with four spades he will bid four spades, knowing that you have the desired eight-card fit.

QUIZ

1. What do you open these hands (i) when non-vulnerable; (ii) when vulnerable?

a. ♠ K 8 7 5   b. ♠ 9 7 6   c. ♠ A Q   d. ♠ A J 7
   ♡ 10 8 6   ♡ A Q J 8 6   ♡ K J 10 5   ♡ 10 7 5
   ◊ A Q J 3   ◊ A 6   ◊ A J 6 5   ◊ A Q 10 7 6
   ♣ K 4   ♣ Q 8 2   ♣ J 8 4   ♣ Q 6

2. What should you respond on these hands when partner has opened (i) a weak no-trump; (ii) a strong no-trump?

a. ♠ 8 6 5   b. ♠ A Q 10 7 6   c. ♠ K J 8 6   d. ♠ Q 10 6 5
   ♡ 6 5   ♡ 8 6 5   ♡ A Q 9 5   ♡ K 6
   ◊ 6 5   ◊ Q J 7   ◊ K 7 5   ◊ 9 6
   ♣ Q 10 9 8 5 4 ♣ 7 3   ♣ 6 4   ♣ A J 9 7 6

3. What is the next bid by you on the following hands after the given auctions? You are sitting West and you are non-vulnerable.

a. ♠ K J 10 7   *West*   *East*
   ♡ A Q 7 5   1NT   2♣
   ◊ 10 8 7   2♡   2NT
   ♣ K 6   ?

b. ♠ A Q 6   *West*   *East*
   ♡ K J 10 7   1NT   2♣
   ◊ 4 3 2   2♡   3♣
   ♣ K J 7   ?

c. ♠ A Q 6   *West*   *East*
   ♡ K J 10 7   1NT   2♣
   ◊ 4 3 2   2♡   3♠
   ♣ K J 7   ?

d. ♠ A Q 6   *West*   *East*
   ♡ 7 5   1NT   2♣
   ◊ K J 10 8   2◊   2♡
   ♣ K 7 6 3   ?

e. ♠ A Q 5	West	East
♡ K 7 6	1♣	1♠
◇ K 6 4	1NT	2♠
♣ K J 5 4	?	

4. Give what you think the auctions ought to be on these hands assuming that West is the dealer and you are vulnerable.

a. *West*   *East*

West	*East*
♠ A 6	♠ 9 7 5 4 3 2
♡ K J 8 6	♡ A 5
◇ A Q 7 5	◇ 6 4 2
♣ K 5 4	♣ J 3

b. *West*	*East*
♠ K 9 8 4	♠ Q 10 6 5
♡ A K J 3	♡ 4 2
◇ 10 8 7	◇ J 6 5 4
♣ A 2	♣ K Q J

c. *West*	*East*
♠ K 7 6 4	♠ A 2
♡ Q J 9 7	♡ 10 5 4
◇ A K 8	◇ 7 4
♣ K 4	♣ A Q 10 6 5 3

d. *West*	*East*
♠ K J	♠ A Q 7 6 4 3 2
♡ 10 7 6	♡ 5
◇ A Q J 8	◇ K 6 4
♣ K Q 7 4	♣ 8 5

e. *West*	*East*
♠ A 2	♠ K J 9 7 5
♡ A 10 8	♡ K J 9 7 5
◇ A K J 7 4	◇ Q 6
♣ 10 6 2	♣ 4

Answers on page 185

5 The Responder's First Bid

I do not object to Gladstone's always having the ace
of trumps up his sleeve, but only to his pretence that
God had put it there.

Henry Labouchere

Your partner has opened the bidding with one of a suit, the next
opponent has passed and now it is up to you. What do you bid? The
first thing to know is that you should only bid with some values, but
you do not need nearly as many points as you would have done to
open the bidding. You should pass your partner's opening bid with less
than six points.

Given that you are not going to pass, your bid falls into one of two
categories: *limit bids* and *unlimited bids*. It has always been a cornerstone of the Acol system that one makes a limit bid as quickly as
possible. A limit bid is one that defines your strength within a close
range. We have already seen one example of a limit bid: the one no-
trump opening bid, showing either 12-14 points non-vulnerable, or
15-17 when vulnerable. The responder should try to make a limit bid

if he can do so.

There are two limit bids that the responder can make directly opposite his partner's opening bid: some number of no-trumps, or a raise of partner's suit.

One No-Trump

This response shows a balanced hand of 6-9 points and denies a four-card or longer suit between, i.e. higher-ranking than, the suit your partner opened and one no-trump.

For example, your partner has opened one diamond and you have to decide what to bid on the following hands.

a. ♠ A 10 7   b. ♠ K J 6 4   c. ♠ Q J 7 5
   ♡ 7 6 4   ♡ A 6 3   ♡ Q J 7 6
   ◇ J 7 4   ◇ 10 6   ◇ 9 6
   ♣ K 6 5 3   ♣ 9 7 6 4   ♣ Q 7 5

The first is an ideal one no-trump response, but with hand *b* you have four spades, a suit between the one opened, diamonds, and one no-trump. As you will see in a minute, one spade is the correct bid on this hand. Deal *c* contains not one but two four-card suits between the bid suit and one no-trump, making one no-trump a doubly bad bid. In this case you will see that one follows the principle used in opening the bidding when holding only four-card suits: you bid them in ascending order, so you respond one heart with this hand.

Two No-Trumps

Being one level higher than one no-trump, this bid shows a few more points. It indicates a balanced hand with no four-card or longer suit between the suit opened and no-trumps and 10-12 points. With which of these hands would you respond two no-trumps to an opening bid of one heart by your partner?

d. ♠ J 7 6 4   e. ♠ J 6 5   f. ♠ 10 8
   ♡ Q 6   ♡ J 8 5   ♡ Q 7 5 4
   ◇ A K 6 5   ◇ K Q 10 5   ◇ K J 6
   ♣ J 6 5   ♣ A 7 4   ♣ A J 10 5

The correct answer is: only *e*. Hand *d* contains four spades, so you should bid one spade; hand *f* has four-card support for the heart suit, so you should be supporting your partner's hearts as you know you have at least an eight-card fit.

Three No-Trumps

As if you could not guess, this shows a balanced hand, denies a four-card or longer suit between the opened suit and no-trumps, and promises 13-15 points. Which of these hands is a three no-trump response to an opening bid of one diamond?

g. ♠ K J 7 5 4	h. ♠ Q 10 7	i. ♠ J 6 4
♡ Q 10 6	♡ A Q J	♡ J 6 5
◇ A Q 2	◇ K 6 3	◇ K Q 8
♣ Q 8	♣ Q 10 7 6	♣ A Q 10 5

Hand *g* certainly does not qualify because it has a five-card spade suit which must be shown, but it is correct to respond three no-trumps with either *h* or *i*.

If you have more than fifteen points, you must find a different bid; four no-trumps, as you see in chapter twelve, is another of those conventional bids.

Now let us consider the hands when you have at least four-card support for the suit in which your partner opened. Here there is a slight difference depending on whether he opened with one of a minor or one of a major.

As I have said before, you try to find the magic eight-card fit, but as you need to be able to take eleven tricks to make game in a minor, it is better to try to locate a major-suit fit, or to investigate the possibilities of playing in no-trumps, when only nine tricks are needed to make game, rather than committing your side irreversibly to playing in a minor. The one qualification to make before raising a minor: always bid a four-card or longer major at the one level if you have one. Otherwise what I will write now can be followed without qualms.

A Single Raise

This is when you bid two of the suit opened by your partner; you raise the bidding by one level. The bid, like one no-trump, promises 6-9 points, but you are allowed to add some distributional points as soon as you know you have a four-four fit. (In fact this is not imperative, and you will not be far wrong if you ignore this bit.) You can add one point for having a doubleton in a side-suit, two points for a singleton, and three points for a void. The reason for this is that you will be able to use your trumps to ruff partner's losers in these side-suits.

Which of these hands should raise a one heart opening bid to two
hearts?

j. ♠ K Q 8   k. ♠ Q 10 9 8   l. ♠ 8 6 3
    ♡ Q J 9 7   ♡ K J 7 4   ♡ K J 5 4
    ◇ 10 6 4 2   ◇ Q 8 4   ◇ K Q 7 6
    ♣ 8 6   ♣ 7 5   ♣ 8 6

Holding hand *j* you have a good raise to two hearts, with eight high-
card points and one distributional point if you are considering your
doubleton. Hand *k* should also bid two hearts. Admittedly you have
four spades, but once you have found a known eight-card or longer fit
in one major, do not worry about the other one. Finally, with hand *l*
you are a little strong for two hearts as you have nine high-card points
and a distributional point for the doubleton, but it is one of the grey
areas that arise in bridge fairly often. No-one can say that it is completely wrong to bid two hearts on those cards. If you want to count
the distributional points, do so and make the next bid listed, three
hearts. But if you wish to ignore them, feeling you have enough to
worry about as it is, just bid two hearts.

That covers raising a major, but what if you have four-card or longer
support for your partner's opening bid of one of a minor? Here it is
right to raise to the two level unless you have a four-card or longer
major, in which case you should bid that major to investigate the
possible fit before supporting partner's minor if he shows no interest
in your suit. Which of these hands should raise one diamond to two
diamonds?

m.♠ Q 10 5 4   n. ♠ K 6 5   o. ♠ 9 7 6
    ♡ 6 5   ♡ 8 6   ♡ 4 2
    ◇ K Q 5 3   ◇ Q 9 7 5   ◇ K Q 6 5
    ♣ 7 4 2   ♣ K 5 3 2   ♣ K 7 6 4

Hand *m* should respond one spade, not two diamonds, because you
might have a four-four major-suit fit. Hand *n* is an ideal two diamond
bid, as is hand *o*.

A Double Raise
This follows the same principle as the two no-trump response: four-
card support and 10-12 points. (Again count the distributional points if
you wish. And show a four-card or longer major before raising the

minor.)

What would you bid over (i) a one diamond opener; (ii) a one heart opener, with these hands?

p. ♠ 7 6 4	q. ♠ K 7 6 4	r. ♠ K 7 6
♡ Q 10 7 6	♡ Q 10 7 6	♡ K 6 5
◇ K J 5 4	◇ K 4	◇ K Q 9 4
♣ A J	♣ K 9 5	♣ 8 7 5

With hand *p* respond one heart over one diamond to show the four-card major; but bid three hearts if partner began with one heart. Holding hand *q* bid one heart over one diamond, four-card suits up the line (in ascending order); but raise one heart to three hearts. Hand *r* should bid three diamonds over one diamond to show the four-card support, but should bid two no-trumps over one heart, as we saw above.

Triple Raise

I just know that you are never going to guess what this bid shows when you raise one of a major to four of the same major. Do I hear you suggesting 13-15 points with at least four-card support? Right! The only thing to remember with this bid is that it might be distributional. For example, suppose you hold ♠ K 8 7 6 5 3 ♡ 4 ◇ Q 10 7 6 4 ♣ 6. Partner opens one spade; which contract would you like him to play in? Yes, four spades. You have few losers even though you do not have many high-card points. Of course, counting distribution, you do have twelve total points (five high-card points, two length points in spades, one in diamonds and four shortage points for the doubletons because you are raising partner's suit). So whenever you get twelve distributional points with a hand that looks as though it should make ten tricks in spades (or hearts), bid four. For one thing, it makes it much harder for the opposition to come into the bidding. On this hand, for example, it is quite possible that both sides can make a game because there are so many distributional points around.

When you raise one of a minor to four of a minor you should not have 13-15 high-card points because it is too likely that you have just gone past the most likely game contract: three no-trumps. You should restrict this bid to a distributional raise holding something like ♠ 7 ♡ 4 ◇ K Q 10 6 5 3 2 ♣ J 6 4 3. When holding a hand with thirteen high-card points, either contemplate bidding three no-trumps, assuming you do not have a four-card major to show, or bid the other minor, in which you must have some length if you do not have a balanced hand or a major, and hope that partner will bid no-trumps, or indicate that in fact five of a minor is not such a bad spot after all.

Unlimited Bids

Most of the time you will find that you cannot make a limited bid, and so you make one that is unlimited: in other words you could have a lot of points and so partner is not allowed to pass — the bid is *forcing*.

If you respond at the one level in a suit it shows at least six points, but it could be quite a strong hand. However, partner assumes the minimum and you bid more later in the auction if you have extra points.

If you bid at the two level without making a jump you show a minimum of nine points, the extra trick needed requiring a minimum of three more points. (If you think about it, there are a total of 40 high-card points in the pack and if they are divided by thirteen, the total number of tricks, it gives three points per trick. So to respond at the two level you need three points more than to bid at the one level if you have a complete minimum. Of course, you might have far more points than that, but partner assumes the minimum.)

Some examples; what do you bid opposite partner's one heart opening bid with these hands?

s. ♠ Q 9 7 6	t. ♠ K J 8 6	u. ♠ A 10 8 7	v. ♠ J 9 7
♡ 8 6 5	♡ 8 5 4	♡ 6 4	♡ 6
◇ 9 5 3 2	◇ A 7 3	◇ 6 3	◇ KQJ53
♣ 8 6	♣ 9 5 4	♣ K 9 7 5 4	♣ A 8 6 5

Hand *s* has only two points, so it is not strong enough to make any bid — just pass. With *t* you make the simple response of one spade showing at least four spades and at least six points. Holding *u* you must also bid one spade. Even though clubs is the longer suit, you do not have nine points, so you cannot bid at the two level. But you want to keep the bidding open, so show your four-card spade suit. In fact if there is any chance for you to make game on this hand, your partner will have to be very strong (18 or 19 points) and either have a good spade fit or be able to make three no-trumps. Unless partner can show a good hand with at least four clubs you are very unlikely to be able to collect eleven tricks in clubs, which you would have to do to make game there.

Hand *v* is an ideal two level response: bid two diamonds. At least nine points and a good suit, and as usual you bid your longest suit first.

What if you have a very strong hand? If you have at least sixteen total points you are allowed to make a single jump into a new suit (what is commonly known as a *jump shift*). But this should show only one of three types of hand:

  (i) a balanced sixteen or more points, or

 (ii) a strong hand with a good one-suiter which you have just bid, or

(iii) a strong hand with two suits, the one you have just bid and the one your partner opened.

— A JUMP SHIFT —

Consider these three hands, partner having opened one diamond.

w. ♠ A K J 9   x. ♠ 9 7   y. ♠ A K J 9 8
    ♡ K Q 10   ♡ A Q J 9 7 6   ♡ 5 4
    ♢ Q 9 5   ♢ A 6   ♢ K Q 10 6
    ♣ K 5 2   ♣ K J 5   ♣ A 3

On the first you are too strong to respond three no-trumps, which shows 13-15 points, and you cannot bid four no-trumps because it is conventional, not natural. So the answer is that you bid two spades, a jump into a new suit as you could have responded one spade. You will then bid no-trumps on the next round and partner will expect a balanced hand with four, or perhaps five, spades and sixteen to about nineteen points. (With twenty opposite his minimum of thirteen you already know you have enough for a slam and so should be heading that way. I will look at slam bidding in a special chapter.)

Holding hand *x* you jump to two hearts, proposing to rebid the heart suit on the next round. Partner will know you have at least six hearts and at least sixteen total points. Hopefully he can work out the best contract.

With hand *y* you bid two spades on the first round and support diamonds on the second, telling partner that you have at least nine cards in the two suits and at least sixteen total points. Again hopefully he will have some idea of where you should be going.

QUIZ

1. What response do you give to a one diamond opening bid with these hands?

a. ♠ K J 6
♡ Q 10 4
◇ 7 5 4
♣ Q 7 5 3

b. ♠ K J 6
♡ 9 7 6
◇ K J 10 6 5 4
♣ 5

c. ♠ K Q J 6
♡ A 4
◇ A Q 7 5 4 3
♣ 6

d. ♠ A K 10
♡ Q 10 5
◇ Q 6 4
♣ K J 6 4

e. ♠ 5
♡ J 9 6
◇ A Q 8 7 4
♣ K 8 6 5

f. ♠ K 10 6
♡ Q 5 3
◇ Q 7 4
♣ K J 7 2

g. ♠ 8 7
♡ Q 6 5
◇ K 7 5 3 2
♣ Q 4 3

h. ♠ Q 10 7 6
♡ K 8
◇ Q 10 5 4
♣ 10 5 4

2. What response do you give to a one heart opening bid with these hands?

a. ♠ K 7
♡ A J 9 4
◇ K 10 7 6
♣ 7 6 5

b. ♠ K Q 10 6
♡ A Q J 9 8
◇ A 3 2
♣ 5

c. ♠ J 9 5
♡ 8 5 3
◇ K J 6 4 2
♣ A Q

d. ♠ 6
♡ K J 8 7 5 4
◇ Q 10 7 6 4
♣ 8

e. ♠ Q 8 6
♡ 7 6
◇ Q 8 7 4
♣ Q J 7 4

f. ♠ K J 6
♡ Q 6
◇ A J 8 2
♣ Q 9 6 4

g. ♠ K J 7 6
♡ Q 10 7 6
◇ 7 5 3
♣ 10 8

h. ♠ A 10 6
♡ K Q 6 4
◇ K J 6 3
♣ 3 2

Answers on page 186

6   *The Opener's First Rebid*

He that plays the king shall be welcome; his majesty
shall have tribute of me.

William Shakespeare

The opener has made his first bid and the responder has replied. Now it
is the time for the opener to rebid, which he must do opposite an
unlimited response, but he may judge that it is best to pass opposite a
limit bid. Let us consider these limit bids first.

One No-Trump Response
Your partner has shown a balanced 6-9 points without four cards in
any suit between the opening suit and no-trumps. You must add your
points to those that he has shown and that will allow you to assess the
potential for the two hands. If you have a balanced hand with eighteen
or nineteen points, bid three no-trumps. At the worst your combined
holding will be only 24 points and your partner will have to play the
cards well, but it could be as high as 28, when you must be in game.

With a balanced seventeen, raise to two no-trumps. This is like the
raise of a one no-trump opening bid to two no-trumps: the responder
raises to three no-trumps with a maximum: a 'good' eight or nine points.

With less points and a balanced hand, just pass. There is no benefit
in playing in two no-trumps rather than one no-trump.

When you have an unbalanced hand you will normally try to bid a
new suit, assuming it is lower-ranking than your original one, or rebid
your own suit if you have at least six cards in it.

Consider these examples after one spade–one no-trump:

a. ♠ K J 10 7 6   b. ♠ A K 8 7 6 5   c. ♠ A Q J 7 6   d. ♠ K Q 6 5
   ♡ Q 10 6   ♡ A Q 10 5   ♡ 8 6   ♡ K J 5
   ◇ A J 8   ◇ 6 3   ◇ K Q 5   ◇ A Q 7
   ♣ A 5   ♣ 2   ♣ K J 9   ♣ K J 9

With *a* just pass one no-trump; you have no reason to suppose that spades will be better. Holding *b* rebid two hearts, showing at least five spades as you have bid a second suit and at least four hearts. With *c* raise to two no-trumps, showing seventeen points (remember the point for the fifth spade). Hand *d* is worth a direct jump to three no-trumps.

What if you have an unbalanced hand and think that you might make a game? In that case you must jump on the second round. A jump rebid of your suit is non-forcing but invitational. For example, if you open one heart holding ♠ 6 5 ♡ A Q 10 7 6 5 ◇ A K J ♣ J 5 and partner responds one no-trump, you want to play in game if partner has a maximum, but not if he has a minimum. The answer is to rebid three hearts, asking him to bid on with a maximum.

A jump into a new suit is forcing because *a new suit at the three level is always forcing*. So with a very strong hand like ♠ 7 6 ♡ A K J 10 6 ◇ A Q J 6 ♣ A 7, after one heart–one no-trump, rebid three diamonds. As before, this promises at least four diamonds, shows that you have at least five hearts, and is forcing. If partner rebids three hearts, raise to four. If he bids three no-trumps because he does not like your suits, pass and hope that he can make nine tricks.

Two No-Trump Response

A similar scheme applies here except that, as I just said, a new suit at the three level is always forcing. Suppose you hold hand *b* given above. Over one no-trump you rebid two hearts, which partner can pass if he prefers hearts to spades and has no reason to raise. However, over a two no-trump response you would rebid three hearts and partner must bid again.

A rebid of your own suit at the three level, though, is a *sign-off*, telling partner that you have heard about his hand and, given that information, you think that the right contract is what you have just bid.

What would you bid with these hands after one heart–two no-trumps?

e. ♠ J 6	f. ♠ 6 5	g. ♠ A Q 4 2
♡ A Q 9 7 6	♡ A J 10 5 4	♡ K J 7 6
◇ K 7 6	◇ K Q 10 6	◇ A Q 7
♣ Q 8 7	♣ A 5	♣ K 8

Pass with *e*; you have only thirteen points, including one for the fifth heart, and so the maximum is 25, not enough to consider trying to make nine tricks. Just hope that he brings home eight.

Holding *f* rebid three diamonds. This shows that you have at least five hearts and at least four diamonds, and is forcing. Note that the doubleton spade is bad for three no-trumps because you know your partner has at most three spades, meaning that there is a risk the opponents will be able to run the spade suit in no-trumps. With luck partner will have three hearts and will be able to support the suit now that he knows you have five.

Hand *g* should just raise to three no-trumps. Even though you have nineteen points, that means that your maximum combined total is only 31, not enough for a slam. Be happy that your partner should have no difficulty in making nine tricks.

Three No-Trump Response

Responding to this bid is straightforward too. A new suit below the level of game is forcing and shows that you have a two-suiter. A rebid into your own major is non-forcing, saying that you prefer to play in that game (four hearts or four spades) rather than three no-trumps. However, to repeat your minor at the four level is forcing. (If you have a weak opener with a long minor, pass three no-trumps and hope he makes it. The bonus for making a game justifies taking the risk.)

The only auction where a new suit shown without a jump is not forcing occurs after a one spade opener. If the rebid following three no-trumps is four hearts, that is just asking partner to select the major-suit game which he prefers.

You open one spade on the following hands and partner responds three no-trumps; what do you bid?

h. ♠ A K J 7 6	i. ♠ A K 8 7 6	j. ♠ K Q 10 8 7
♡ Q 4 3	♡ K Q 6 5 2	♡ 6 5
◇ K 5	◇ 4 2	◇ A K J 10 7
♣ 10 7 6	♣ 5	♣ A

Holding hand *h* you should pass three no-trumps. You both have balanced hands and the strong spade suit will produce at least four tricks, so he should be able to bring in nine tricks. You have no reason to suppose that four spades will be better.

With hand *i* bid four hearts, asking partner to say whether he would prefer that you play in four spades or four hearts. Clearly it would be wrong with those two good suits and the very weak minors to pass three no-trumps.

Hand *j* has a lot of potential if partner has a fit for one or both of your suits. You already know of at least a combined point total of 32 points, excluding the two you will be able to add for your singleton if partner can fit one or both of your suits. Clearly there is more than a faint aroma of a slam in the air. Four diamonds is forcing and it is up to your partner to tell you which suit he likes.

A Single Raise

If you have opened one of a minor and partner has raised to the two level, the only possible game contract will normally be three no-trumps. If you have a balanced nineteen points, bid three no-trumps; if you have a balanced 17 or 18, bid two no-trumps, asking partner to go on to game with a maximum. With less points than seventeen, just pass. You are very unlikely to be able to make game.

With an unbalanced hand only move on if you really can visualise game. Bid a second suit, or raise to three of the minor as a *game-try*.

For example, what do you bid on these hands after partner has raised your one diamond opening bid to two diamonds?

k. ♠ A J 9   l. ♠ Q 10 6
  ♡ K Q 10   ♡ K J 5
  ◇ K 9 8 4   ◇ K Q 9 8
  ♣ A Q 4   ♣ A J 6

m. ♠ K Q 10 7   n. ♠ K Q 10
  ♡ A   ♡ A J 7
  ◇ K Q 10 6 5 3 ◇ A Q 10 8 7 6
  ♣ K 4   ♣ 5

With hand *k* bid three no-trumps and with *l* pass. With *m* go two spades even though you know partner does not have four spades. It is possible that you can make either three no-trumps or five diamonds, so show him where you have length. Unfortunately with hand *n* you do not have another suit to show him, so raise to three diamonds to tell him that you have an interest in game, not a balanced hand because you have not bid no-trumps, and no second suit to show. This means you are almost certain to have at least six diamonds.

If partner has raised one of a major to two of the major, things are slightly different because the ten trick target for game is more likely. This time you bid another suit to show length, but partner is being asked to see if he can help out in that suit: either a couple of honour cards, or a singleton so that opener's losers in the suit can be ruffed are ideal holdings.

Again a single raise to the three level denies a second suit and is inviting game if partner has a maximum.

What do you bid with these hands after partner has raised one heart to two hearts?

o. ♠ A Q	p. ♠ K J 9 8	q. ♠ K J 8	r. ♠ 6 5 4
♡ K Q 10 8 3	♡ A K 8 5 4	♡ A Q 10 7 6 5	♡ A K 8 7 6
◇ K 7 6	◇ A 6 5	◇ A 8 5	◇ A 9 7 5
♣ A 7 2	♣ 6	♣ 9	♣ A

With *o* just bid four hearts. You know of a combined minimum of 26 points, counting your distributional and shortage points. This is enough for game so just bid it.

Holding hand *p* you can envisage a game if partner has a maximum, so show your second suit with a bid of two spades. Hand *q* has eighteen points including the distributional values, so raise to three hearts asking partner to go on with a maximum (eight or nine points). Hand *r* also has eighteen points, so bid three diamonds to show your second suit and tell partner that you have an interest in game if his hand fits a red two-suiter.

A Double Raise

This follows the same principles except that as partner has shown more points, you will be able to bid on with less. Also, if he has raised a major to the three level, there is no room below the level of game to make a game-try. Either you bid game or you stop in the partscore; you cannot get any help in making the decision from your partner.

If partner has raised a minor, you might be able to make three no-trumps or five of the minor, so you can bid majors to show values in those suits, asking partner to say which game contract he prefers.

Here are a few more examples. What do you bid after one spade-three spades?

s. ♠ A J 7 6 5	t. ♠ A Q 7 5 3	u. ♠ K J 9 6 5
♡ K 7 5	♡ A K 6	♡ A K
◇ K 5 4	◇ K J 7	◇ J 7
♣ J 7	♣ 9 6	♣ A K 8 7

You have a complete minimum with hand *s* so you should pass and hope you make nine tricks. Holding *t* you have a nice hand but it is unlikely you will be able to make a slam, so just raise to four spades, expecting to make it fairly easily. However, with *u* it is not difficult to visualise a slam, so bid four clubs to show your second suit and hope that partner has better than a minimum with some useful honours in diamonds and spades.

A Triple Raise

If partner has just raised your one of a minor opening bid to the four level, you know that he has a weak hand with a lot of trumps. You can bid on to game if you think you can make eleven tricks, but otherwise pass, hoping you can make your contract, or that the opposition have been talked out of bidding when they could have made something.

If partner has raised one of a major to the game level you will usually pass. But if you think you might be able to make a slam, you can move on. However, I am doing a separate chapter just on bidding slams, and so I will consider the different possibilities then.

Now we move on to the more awkward situations when partner has made an unlimited bid. However, the standard principles apply: bid a second suit if you can to show at least five in your first suit and at least four in your second; bid no-trumps to show a balanced hand; raise his suit if you know of at least an eight-card fit; and make a jump bid if you have better than a minimum (in this case normally seventeen or more points, or a good sixteen). Let us look at a few examples, assuming you have opened one diamond and partner has responded one heart.

A. ♠ A Q 4
♡ K 6 5
♢ K J 7 4
♣ K 8 6

B. ♠ 6 5 3
♡ K J 8 7
♢ K J 9 8 3
♣ A

C. ♠ K J 10 6
♡ A 3
♢ Q J 10 4 2
♣ K 6

D. ♠ A 3
♡ K 9 7 6
♢ K Q 9 7 6
♣ K 7

E. ♠ 8 6 5
♡ 6
♢ A Q 9 6 5
♣ K Q J 7

F. ♠ K J 8
♡ Q 8 5
♢ A K J 7
♣ K J 7

G. ♠ A 6
♡ A J 8 7
♢ A Q 9 8 7
♣ 8 5

H. ♠ 6
♡ K J 7
♢ A K J 8 5
♣ A Q 10 7

Did you wonder what the vulnerability is with hand *A*? If so, you should have known! If you were vulnerable you would open this hand with one no-trump, not one diamond, so you must be non-vulnerable. The correct rebid, of course, is one no-trump, as we found out in chapter five.

Hand *B* has fifteen points including distribution, so it is not worth a jump. As you have four hearts you know of at least an eight-card fit, so you should raise to two hearts.

Hand *C* should continue the natural development of the auction by bidding one spade, promising at least five diamonds and at least four spades.

Holding *D* you have nineteen total points. Add that to your partner's minimum of six and you know that you have at least 25 – virtually enough for game. So you should bid four hearts. When you can see the eight-card fit and enough values for games, do not beat about the bush.

Hand *E* is similar to *C* except that your second suit is clubs, so rebid two clubs.

Hand *F* is a text-book two no-trump rebid to show seventeen or eighteen points and a balanced hand.

Hand *G* has a total of eighteen points, so you should jump to three hearts. If partner has better than a minimum six or seven points he will go on to four hearts and you should be confident he will make it.

Hand *H* has nineteen points, including one for the fifth diamond but nothing for the singleton spade as no eight-card fit has been found yet, and so you must make a jump rebid. In this case three clubs is clearly correct because it shows at least five diamonds and at least four clubs.

If partner has responded at the two level the bidding continues in the same way, just a level higher. No-trump bids we have covered, and all other bids are natural, jumps being made with the extra values. Consider on these hands that you have opened one spade and partner has responded two clubs. What do you bid?

I. ♠ A K J 10 7 6	J. ♠ K Q 10 8	K. ♠ A K J 8 7
♡ K Q 5	♡ A J 8	♡ K Q J 9 4
◇ Q 7 4	◇ K J 7	◇ K 6
♣ 6	♣ J 7 6	♣ 5
L. ♠ K J 9 5 3	M. ♠ K Q 9 6 4	N. ♠ A J 9 7 6
♡ A 8	♡ 8 7	♡ K J 9
◇ K Q 7 6	◇ A 5	◇ A Q 6
♣ 9 5	♣ K J 7 6	♣ K 7
O. ♠ A K 10 7 6	P. ♠ K J 10 7 6 5	
♡ A 8 7	♡ A Q 6	
◇ 6	◇ Q 9	
♣ K J 7 6	♣ 6 3	

Hand *I* has seventeen points counting the length in spades, and partner's response at the two level guarantees at least nine. You are in the game region, but the lack of fit for partner should make you a little cautious. If you have a singleton in the first suit your partner bids it is a disadvantage and there is a case for subtracting one point from your hand evaluation. (But if you think all this addition and subtraction is getting beyond a joke, just stick to the bits that you feel you can handle. Once you become a better player you will find that this sort of hand evaluation adjustment will become almost second nature, like driving a car once you have passed your test.) However, as you have more than a minimum you should make a jump rebid. In this case you do not have a second suit, so you rebid three spades. A jump rebid in the suit opened shows at least a six-card suit, better than a minimum and no other four-card suit in principle. (However, you might ignore a very weak suit when you have a strong six-card suit. For example, if you held something like ♠ A K J 10 7 6 ♡ A Q ◇ J 6 4 3 ♣ 6, it would be sensible to rebid three spades rather than two diamonds.)

Hand *J* is a clear-cut two no-trump rebid to show a balanced fifteen or sixteen points.

Hand *K* has nineteen points counting two length points in the majors, so jump rebid with three hearts to show better than a minimum, at least five spades and at least four hearts.

The next one, *L*, is a simple two diamond rebid to show the second suit, and at the same time indicating less than seventeen points.

What is the club fit on hand *M*? It must be at least eight-cards, so you should raise clubs. As you have a minimum, just bid three clubs. (How many spades will your partner expect you to hold? He knows you have four clubs and if you had only four spades you would have opened one club, the lower suit, not one spade. *Ergo*, you have five or more spades.)

You have a balanced eighteen points on *N*, so rebid three no-trumps. Admittedly you have a fifth spade, but one can open one no-trump with five-card minors, so it might not make any difference. In fact, though, if you open the lower of two four-card suits at the one level, a one spade opener shows at least a five-card suit unless you have specifically 4-3-3-3 distribution.

Hand *O* contains a total of eighteen points in support of clubs. The singleton diamond suggests that three no-trumps is not the right contract, so jump raise to four clubs. You have a combined total of at least 27 points, and so partner will only pass with a dreadful minimum.

(In other books you might read that this jump raise to four of a minor is forcing, but that contravenes Acol principles and is wrong in my opinion.)

Last but not least, hand *P*. You do not have more than a minimum, you do not have a second four-card suit, you do not have four-card club support, so all you can do is rebid your six-card spade suit: say two spades.

The last possibility is that partner has made a jump shift response. In that case you are forced to reach game and so there is no sense in making unnecessary jump bids. You should just make your natural rebid and prepare to bid higher if you do have extra values. Remember that partner has guaranteed at least sixteen points, so if you have eighteen you are already at least in the small slam region.

To take a simple example, reconsider hand *I*. Let us assume that partner responded three clubs to your one spade opener, not two clubs. It would be quite wrong to rebid four spades; just make a simple rebid of three spades and await your partner's next move (either three no-trumps to show the balanced hand, or four clubs to confirm an excellent suit, or four spades with the spade–club two-suiter). You will then make a move towards a slam.

QUIZ

1. You have the following hand: ♠ A Q 6 5 4 ♡ K J 10 7 6 ◇ A 4 ♣ 3. You open one spade; what do you rebid after partner responds:
a. one no-trump b. two clubs c. two spades d. two no-trumps e. three clubs f. three spades g. three no-trumps h. four spades?

Answers on page 186

7 The Responder's First Rebid

'It's a poor sort of memory that only works back-
wards,' the Queen remarked.

Lewis Carroll

As you would expect, the responder tries to make a descriptive rebid
to give the opener further information about the shape and strength
of his hand. If the responder made a limit bid on the first round, he
will normally have little alternative but to accept or refuse a game-try,
or to indicate his preference between two suits bid by the opener.
However, if he has made an unlimited first response, he will try to limit
his hand on the second round. All the limit bids given for the initial
response keep identical meanings on the second round. So, a bid of
one no-trump shows 6-9 points and a stopper in the unbid suit; a two
no-trump rebid, whether as a jump or not, shows 10-12 points; support
for partner's first or second suit follows the identical scheme to that
outlined in Chapter 5, the only difference being that if the opener has
bid two suits, the responder can support the first with only three cards
as he now knows the opener to have at least five in that suit.

If the responder rebids his own suit without jumping it is weak and
shows at least a six-card suit. If he jump rebids his own suit it is invitational, asking partner to go on to game unless he has a misfitting
minimum.

If the opener has rebid his own suit, a change of suit by the responder is not forcing if it is at the one or two level unless it is a reverse
(see Chapter 8). However, a new suit at the three level is always forcing.

Here are some hands that cover all these possibilities.

First of all assume that partner opened one club, you responded one
spade and he rebid two clubs. What do you bid now with these hands?

a. ♠ K 8 6 5 4   b. ♠ A Q 6 4 3   c. ♠ K Q 10 7 6 5 d. ♠ A J 7 6 4
   ♡ 10 7 6   ♡ K J 7 6   ♡ Q 6 5   ♡ K 10 7
   ◇ Q 5 4   ◇ 5 4   ◇ 6 4 3   ◇ Q 10 6
   ♣ Q 6   ♣ 8 4   ♣ 7   ♣ 8 5

e. ♠ Q 10 7 6   f. ♠ A Q 9 8 5   g. ♠ K Q 10 9 6 5 h. ♠ Q 10 7 6 4
   ♡ A 6   ♡ A Q 7 5   ♡ A 3   ♡ A Q 5
   ◇ Q 4   ◇ 8 6   ◇ 6 4   ◇ A J 8
   ♣ J 8 7 5 4   ♣ 6 5   ♣ J 7 4   ♣ 5 4

With *a* you gave a reply with only eight points, counting the fifth
spade, and if your partner cannot jump on the second round, you know
that no game is on. There is a reasonable club fit, so just pass.

Hand *b* might make a game; partner can still hold four hearts in this
auction. The correct bid is two hearts, showing moderate values not
worth a game-force and at least five spades and four or more hearts.

Which contract do you think you can make holding hand *c*? Yes,
two spades must surely be better than two clubs, so rebid it. You have
a good six-card suit and only a singleton club. This bid is weak, so
partner should pass.

Ten high-card points in *d*, a fairly balanced hand and stoppers in the
red suits: rebid two no-trumps. This shows the same number of points
as if you had responded to two no-trumps on the first round.

Twelve points if you count something for the two doubletons, so
raise to three clubs with hand *e*. This shows 10-12 points, the same as if
you had given the double raise on the first round, but this time you do
not need to have four-card trump support; three is sufficient opposite
a known five-card or longer suit. (Note that one spade is the correct
response on the first round, showing the four-card major.)

Thirteen points in hand *f* mean that you have enough for game, so
you must jump to three hearts to force partner to keep bidding. He will
know you have the points for game, at least five spades and at least
four hearts. Hopefully knowing all that he can bid the best game
contract.

Hand *g* is a little more awkward. You have three-card support for
clubs, but you have only shown four spades. That spade suit it reasonably self-supporting, and you have enough points to be able to contract
for game unless partner has a complete minimum. The correct bid is
three spades, which would also be right if you had the same hand without the jack of clubs.

Fourteen points, counting the fifth spade, stoppers in both red suits and basically a balanced hand; all that adds up to a rebid of three no-trumps with *h*. Admittedly partner might have three spades and four spades could be a better contract, but no system has yet been invented (or ever will be) that bids all hands perfectly. One should try to play the percentages, and most of the time three no-trumps will be the correct contract when holding this hand after the stated start to the auction.

Bidding after the first two rounds continues in similar style, but by then hopefully the opener has some idea of where the hand is going. If he knows exactly where to play, he should bid the final contract. Otherwise he makes a bid that leaves partner with some say in the matter.

I hope that gives you some idea of the natural way that the bidding continues using the Acol system. Just show your points and your suits, combine that with what partner is telling you, and try to arrive at a final contract that corresponds with what you know.

QUIZ

1. Partner opens one club, you respond one spade and he rebids one no-trump. What do you bid (i) when not vulnerable; (ii) when vulnerable, on these hands?

a. ♠ A Q 10 9 7 6 4
♡ K J 6
◇ 6 4
♣ 3

b. ♠ K J 8 6 5 4
♡ A 7 6
◇ 7 5
♣ 8 5

c. ♠ Q 10 7 6
♡ K J 8
◇ 8 6 5
♣ K 10 7

d. ♠ A J 8 7 6
♡ K J 8 6
◇ 7
♣ 6 5 3

2. Partner opens one spade, you bid two clubs and he rebids two hearts. What do you bid now with these cards?

a. ♠ 6
♡ Q 7 6
◇ 6 5 4 3
♣ A Q 10 8 7

b. ♠ K 7
♡ Q 9 7 6
◇ 4 3
♣ A 10 7 6 5

c. ♠ K J 8
♡ K 5
◇ 7 6 4
♣ A 8 7 5 4

d. ♠ Q 5
♡ 10 8 7
◇ A Q 7
♣ Q J 10 7 6

e. ♠ 10 7
♡ Q 5
◇ 5 3 2
♣ A J 10 7 6 5

f. ♠ K 7 6
♡ 8 7
◇ 7 6
♣ A J 10 8 7 6

g. ♠ K J 7
♡ K 8
◇ 8 7
♣ A Q 10 7 6 5

h. ♠ Q 4
♡ K J 7 5
◇ 9 7
♣ A J 8 6 5

3. Partner opens one heart, you respond two clubs and he rebids two hearts. What do you bid now with these hands?

a. ♠ 7 6
   ♡ 6 5
   ◇ A Q 7 5
   ♣ A Q J 7 6

b. ♠ 8
   ♡ J 7 6
   ◇ J 5 4 3
   ♣ A Q 10 8 7

c. ♠ 8 6
   ♡ K 8 7
   ◇ K 6
   ♣ K 10 8 7 5 4

d. ♠ K J 7
   ♡ 8 6
   ◇ A Q
   ♣ 10 8 7 5 4 3

Answers on page 186

— THE REVERSE SHOWS EXTRA STRENGTH —

8   *The Reverse*

How absolute the knave is! we must speak by the
card, or equivocation will undo us.
                                    William Shakespeare

There are three facets of constructive bidding that I have carefully
avoided in the preceding chapters. I will cover each in the next three
chapters. They are a bit tougher to grasp than the previous material, so
skip these chapters until you have been playing for a while if you wish.
(Or keep this book with you and ask if you can refer to it if one of
them comes up. Hopefully the opposition will be lenient as they know
you are learning the game.) The first is called the *reverse* because you
bid the suits in *ascending order* at *different* levels. Consider this hand:
♠ A Q 10 8 7 ♡ K Q 6 5 ◇ A Q 7 ♣ 7. You would open one spade
and then rebid in hearts, let us say at the two level because you mis-
counted your points! If partner wants to put you back to your first,
longer suit, he need only bid at the same level as your last bid. In other
words, to rebid in spades he can say two spades because your last bid
was two hearts. But suppose we switch round the majors and make the
hand ♠ K Q 6 5 ♡ A Q 10 8 7 ◇ A Q 7 ♣ 7. Now you open one
heart, and we will assume partner bids two clubs. You show your
second suit with two spades, but do you see the difference? If your
partner wishes to return to your first suit, hearts, he must bid *three*
hearts, one level higher. Because you force your partner to go to a
higher level to show preference for your first suit, you need to have
some extra values to allow for this. It is generally accepted that you
should never reverse with less than sixteen total points. So the above
hand is an acceptable reverse. But if you had
♠ K 5 3 2 ♡ A Q 9 7 2 ◇ K J 8 ♣ 6, you would open one heart
and if partner responded two clubs, you would have to rebid two
hearts, not two spades. There is a slight risk that you will miss a spade
fit, but if partner has four spades, he should bid two spades over two

hearts. (And if he holds something like this:
♠ A Q 6 5 ♡ 8 5 ◇ 9 6 ♣ K 9 8 5 3, which would pass two hearts, he should respond one spade, not two clubs because the major-suit fit must take priority over the minor-suit fit.)

There is one other point: the opener must bid his two suits at different levels. So one can never make a reverse at the one level. To open one club and rebid one spade over a one heart response requires that the responder goes up to the two level to support the opener's first suit, but the opener had no option but to bid his second suit at the one level. That is not a reverse.

So to go through a reverse by the opener again: it guarantees that the first suit is longer than the second, that he has at least sixteen points, preferably more, and that he must bid the suits at different levels. The responder just continues the bidding in the same way as if there had been no reverse except, of course, he can take into account the extra values that the opener has shown.

That is not quite the whole story about an opener's reverse. I have said that it shows at least sixteen points. If the responder has bid at the one level, he has promised only a minimum of six, giving a known total of at least 22 points — not enough for more than a partscore. So the responder is allowed to pass a reverse in this situation. Suppose he holds
♠ K 7 6 5 4 ♡ Q J 6 ◇ 3 ♣ 8 5 4 3. He responds to a one diamond opener with one spade, and the opener rebids two hearts; what bid would you make? You cannot support diamonds, you cannot repeat your spades because that would show six (and, anyway, you do not know that partner has any), and you cannot bid no-trumps because you do not have a stopper in the unbid suit, clubs. Even though you only know about a seven-card heart fit, get out while you can — pass. If the opener has so many points that he can feel sure of game after a one level response, he must make a jump reverse, which is similar to making a jump rebid that is not a reverse. For example, if the opener has, say,
♠ K Q 4 ♡ A Q 9 7 ◇ A K 9 8 7 ♣ 6 after a one diamond opener and a one spade response, he must rebid *three* hearts if he does not want to risk partner passing a two heart reverse. Of course the responder will try to keep the bidding open if he can, but sometimes he will have no option but to pass.

However, now consider the situation after the responder has bid at the two level. Here he has guaranteed at least nine points, and if a reverse promises at least sixteen it gives the partnership a minimum of 25 points — one point short of the requirements for game if both have absolute minimums. So I have always thought that it is best to play a reverse after a two level response as forcing to game. This does not find universal acceptance, but it makes everything so much simpler if both partners realise they are in a game-forcing auction. I recommend that you adopt this proposal, but do not be too surprised if you get the odd funny look from some players who have not read this book and have not thought about the implications of a reverse after a two level response!

Now let us look at the *responder's reverse*. This will occur after the opener has rebid his own suit following the responder's first bid. In this case a bid can be classified as a responder's reverse if the opener has to bid at the *three level* or higher to show simple preference for the responder's first suit. In effect this means that when the responder bids his second suit, he either does it at the three level, when you might think he has not really made a reverse at all, or at the two level in a suit higher than the one in which he made his initial response.

Here are some responder's reverse auctions:

a. Opener	Responder	b. Opener	Responder	c. Opener	Responder
1♣	1♢	1♢	1♡	1♡	2♣
2♣	2♠	2♢	2♠	2♡	3♢

d. Opener	Responder	e. Opener	Responder	f. Opener	Responder
1♢	2♣	1♡	1♠	1♡	2♢
2♢	2♡	2♡	3♣	2♡	3♣

Note that the last two auctions will not be called responder's reverses by many people because to make a reverse one normally has to bid two suits in ascending order, not in descending order like here. But the opener, to give preference to the responder's first suit, spades and diamonds, respectively, must bid at the three level.

As with the opener's reverse, the responder must have extra values to make a reverse. I think that the minimum ought to be a good eleven points. However, the auctions are pretty similar to the ones we have seen before. The opener makes a natural bid, preferably in no-trumps if he has a stopper in the unbid suit, but he should always bear in mind that the responder has promised at least eleven points. I think the easiest way to see how a responder's reverse affects the bidding is to consider a selection of hands.

♠ K 7 4	♠ Q 10 8 6
♡ A K J 7 6	♡ 5 4
◇ 6 4	◇ A K J 7 5
♣ K 10 9	♣ Q 5
Opener	*Responder*
1♡	2◇
2♡	2♠
3NT	No

Opener bids his heart suit, responder shows his longer suit, opener
rebids his five-card heart suit and the responder makes a reverse into his
second suit. As this guarantees at least eleven points, the opener adds
his fifteen and sees that they have enough for game. Along with his club
stopper, he jumps to three no-trumps because a bid of two no-trumps
shows a minimum number of points and can be passed by the responder
if he has a minimum too.

♠ 9 6	♠ K Q 7 5
♡ K 7 4	♡ A Q 8 6 5
◇ A K J 5 4 2	◇ Q 6
♣ 6 4	♣ 3 2
Opener	*Responder*
1◇	1♡
2◇	2♠
3♡	4♡
No	

Three natural bids are followed by the responder's reverse. Now that
the opener knows of the eight-card heart fit, he shows his support and
the responder goes on to game. Note that this three heart bid is not
forcing because both the opener and the responder could have minimums, in which case the combined count would be only 24 points,
not enough for game. So the opener was close to jumping to four
hearts because of his good fit, but his minimum count and four small
cards in the black suits suggest discretion. However, the responder has
some points to spare, so he bids on.

♠ A J 8 7	♠ K Q 6 3
♡ 5 4	♡ 8 7 3
◇ A K J 5 4	◇ 6
♣ 10 7	♣ A K Q 8 6
Opener	*Responder*
1◇	2♣
2◇	2♠
3♠	4♠
No	

The opener bids his longest suit, the responder shows his as well, and then the opener must rebid his diamonds because he does not have enough points to make a reverse. However, the spade fit is not lost because the responder has enough to make his reverse, the opener shows his four-card support and the good game is reached. (Remember that if the responder has this shape without enough points to reverse, for example ♠ K 6 5 3 ♡ 8 7 3 ◇ 6 ♣ A Q 5 4 2, he should respond one spade on the first round, not two clubs. This is the one time the responder bids a shorter suit than his longest in response to an opening bid.)

♠ Q 10 8	♠ A J
♡ A K J 9 8	♡ 10 3
◇ Q 3 2	◇ A K 8 6 5
♣ 6 3	♣ Q 10 9 7
Opener	*Responder*
1♡	2◇
2♡	3♣
3◇	3NT
No	

Three natural bids and then the responder's reverse by my definition. In fact the opener does have a fit for diamonds, which he shows with three diamonds, but as the responder has a spade holding, he suggests that nine tricks might be easier to make than eleven. The opener, with his useful spade support, has no reason to disagree.

QUIZ

1. Which of these auctions feature reverses, either by the opener or the responder?

a. Opener	Responder	b. Opener	Responder	c. Opener	Responder
1♡	2◇	1♣	1♡	1◇	1♡
2♡	2♠	1♠		2◇	2♠

d. Opener	Responder	e. Opener	Responder	f. Opener	Responder
1♣	1◇	1♠	2♡	1◇	1♠
1♡	1♠	2♠	3♣	2◇	2♡

2. Which of these hands are worth reverses by the opener?

a. ♠ K Q 10 9	b. ♠ K 10 8 7	c. ♠ K 10 8
♡ A 2	♡ K J 8 5 4	♡ A Q 9 6 5
◇ K J 7 5 4	◇ A Q	◇ 10 7 6
♣ A 2	♣ 5 4	♣ A K

3. Which of these hands are worth reverses by the responder?

a. ♠ K J 6 5	b. ♠ 9 7	c. ♠ 7 6
♡ 8 7 6	♡ A Q 10 7	♡ 8 7
◇ K 9 7 6 5	◇ K J 10 8 7	◇ A K J 10
♣ 3	♣ J 6	♣ A K 6 4 3

4. What are your suggested auctions for these hands, the opener always being West?

a. West	East	b. West	East
♠ A K J 5 3	♠ 10 8	♠ 6 4 3	♠ 9 8
♡ Q 10 7	♡ J 5	♡ Q 10 8 7	♡ A K 5 3
◇ 6 5	◇ A K Q J 4	◇ A K J 10 6	◇ Q 5
♣ Q 8 7	♣ A K 3 2	♣ A	♣ Q10875

c. West	East
♠ K 4	♠ A 10 7
♡ 5 4	♡ A 9 7 6
◇ K Q 10 8 7 6	◇ 2
♣ A J 4	♣ K Q 10 8 7

Answers on page 187

9   *4-4-4-1 Hands*

Singularity is almost invariably a clue.
                    Sir Arthur Conan Doyle

There is one distribution that I have purposely overlooked in the earlier chapters because it is one that contravenes the idea that if you bid one suit as opener and then a different suit after the responder has replied, you have guaranteed at least five cards in the first suit. When you have the dreaded 4-4-4-1 shape, with any of the four possible singletons, this rule breaks down. What is worse, partner will never bid assuming that you have 4-4-4-1 and so you can occasionally land in a bad contract with an inadequate trump fit. If that happens to you, just grin and bear it.

The simplest rule is that you *open the suit below your singleton* unless you have 4-4-4-1 shape (a singleton club), in which case you start with one heart.

Let us consider each one in turn. First of all 1-4-4-4 shape, the one with a singleton spade. If partner responds one spade, as you expect, rebid two clubs. But if he bids a minor, raise to the level dictated by the strength of your hand.

With 4-1-4-4 shape start with one diamond. If the responder bids one heart, continue with one spade. The responder will expect at least five diamonds for this rebid but, as I have said, you cannot have everything.

Holding 4-4-1-4, open the bidding with one club. If partner bids one diamond, rebid one heart and again slightly mislead your partner about your club length. Of course, if he is a good partner, not one who is always putting you in a jam, he will respond one heart or one spade and you can raise to the appropriate level.

Finally, with 4-4-4-1 shape open one heart. This gives you the best chance of finding a fit in either major. If he responds one spade, raise to the correct level. If he bids two clubs, though, rebid two diamonds. Of course, if he bids two diamonds, raise.

That is the simple way to deal with these awkward hands. The only saving grace with them is that about 80% of the time you will have at least one fit that is four-four or better.

(In the sequel to this book I will propose an alternative selection of opening bids with these hands, but it is better when you are starting to stick to something that works reasonably well and is easy to remember. Later on, when you have got some experience and most of the bidding comes quite naturally, then is the time to start worrying about more complicated methods.)

QUIZ

1. What is your opening bid on these hands?

a.	♠ K J 9 8	b.	♠ K Q 6 5	c.	♠ K 10 6 5
	♡ 6		♡ A Q 10 5		♡ Q J 9 8
	◇ A Q 9 7		◇ 7		◇ A Q 10 4
	♣ K 10 6 5		♣ K 6 4 2		♣ 8

2. You open the following hand with one heart:
♠ 8 ♡ A K J 10 ◇ A Q J 10 ♣ 5 4 3 2. What do you rebid over the following responses by your partner?
a. one spade   b. one no-trump   c. two clubs   d. two diamonds
e. two hearts.

Answers on page 187

— THE SUIT BELOW THE SINGLETON —

10   *Fourth Suit Forcing*

Let spades be trumps! she said, and trumps they were.

Alexander Pope

Now we get to the hardest bit of all. I recommend that you skip this chapter to begin with, and come back to it after you have been playing for a while. I could have left it out altogether, but it is such an important part of good constructive bidding that I feel the book would be incomplete without it. This will be quite a simple exposé of *fourth suit forcing*: the sequel can have a complete outline of all the things you can do with the 'gadget'.

The simplest way to start is to consider an example. Suppose you pick up ♠ A J 9 7 6 ♡ 9 7 6 ◇ K 2 ♣ K J 8, your partner opens one diamond, you respond one spade and he bids two clubs; what do you bid now? You have thirteen points, which is enough for game, but which game will you play in? Your partner might hold any of these hands:

a. ♠ K Q 5	b. ♠ 10	c. ♠ 5
♡ 4	♡ K Q 10	♡ A 5
◇ A Q 8 7 5	◇ A Q J 8 7	◇ A J 10 8 6
♣ Q 10 5 4	♣ Q 10 6 5	♣ A 10 7 6 5

Opposite *a* you wish to play in four spades; opposite *b* the correct game is three no-trumps; and opposite *c* five clubs is the spot. How can you guess which hand your partner is holding? The answer is that at the moment you cannot. The solution to the problem is to bid the fourth suit. This is an artificial bid telling your partner that you have enough for game but that you cannot say which game you should be in. You are asking your partner to describe his hand further so that you can judge which game you should bid. *It does not promise any length in the suit bid*.

74

— FOURTH SUIT FORCING —

Considering the above hands opposite the original one for the responder, in each case the bidding begins 1◇-1♠-2♣ and then the responder bids two hearts, the fourth suit (the only one unbid at that point). The opener must say what he has. With *a* he shows his spade support with two spades (remember that he has already denied four-card support by failing to raise immediately, so he is now indicating three-card support), and the responder will then bid four spades.

Holding *b* the opener should rebid two no-trumps to show the heart stoppers, over which the responder will raise to three no-trumps.

Finally, with *c* the opener rebids three clubs to show that he is at least five-five in the minors. (To bid a suit once promises only four, to bid it a second time indicates at least five, and to introduce a new suit after you have already bid one indicates that the first suit contains at least five cards — so to bid diamonds and then clubs twice promises at least five cards in both minors.)

Having looked at those examples we can list the requirements for using fourth suit forcing:

(i) enough points for game — a 'good' twelve or more;

(ii) an uncertainty as to the correct game contract;

(iii) five (or more) cards in the first suit that you, the responder, bid;

(iv) usually no stopper in the fourth suit because otherwise you would bid no-trumps.

If your partner uses fourth suit forcing, you, the opener, should try to bid no-trumps if holding a stopper in the fourth suit. Failing that, support partner's first suit if you can, remembering that he should have five cards in that suit. If neither of those is a possibility, make your own natural rebid, showing a five-five, or rebidding your original suit if you are six-four, or raising the fourth suit if you have either 4-4-4-1 or 5-4-4-0 shape.

You open one heart, partner bids one spade, you rebid two clubs, and he bids two diamonds, fourth suit. What do you bid with each of these hands?

d. ♠ 8 3
♡ A 9 7 5 4
◇ A Q
♣ K 9 6 5

e. ♠ 6
♡ K Q 7 5 4
◇ 8 6
♣ A K J 7 6

f. ♠ K 7 6
♡ Q 10 7 5 4
◇ 4
♣ A K 8 5

g. ♠ K Q 6
♡ A K J 7 6
◇ 7
♣ Q 9 7 6

h. ♠ 5
♡ K J 8 7
◇ A Q 10 7
♣ K 10 9 7

With the first you should rebid two no-trumps, showing a hand with at least one, and preferably two, diamond stoppers. (If you had a couple more points you would be allowed to jump to three no-trumps to tell your partner the good news.) Hand *e* rebids three clubs to show the five-five; and *f* is a classic two spade rebid to indicate your three-card support to partner. Hand *g* looks as though it might rebid two spades as well, but can you see the difference in strength between the two hands? The first (*f*) has only twelve high-card points, whereas the second (*g*) has fifteen, so you should tell your partner that you have better than a minimum with three-card spade support by jumping to three spades. (Compare that with the possibility of jumping to three no-trumps mentioned above.) Finally, hand *h* raises the fourth suit to show the 1-4-4-4 or 0-5-4-4 shape; the responder can then make his own arrangements.

QUIZ

1. Which of these hands should make a fourth suit forcing bid of two spades after 1♡-2♣-2◇?

a. ♠ K J 6
   ♡ 6 5
   ◇ Q 8 7
   ♣ A K 10 7 6

b. ♠ K 8 7 6
   ♡ 7 6
   ◇ 8 6
   ♣ K Q 8 6 5

c. ♠ 9 8 5
   ♡ 9 8
   ◇ K J 6
   ♣ A K Q 10 7

d. ♠ 5 4
   ♡ Q 6
   ◇ 7 6 5
   ♣ A K 10 8 7 5

2. What do you bid after the auction has started 1◇-1♠-2♣-2♡ when holding the following hands?

a. ♠ 6 4
   ♡ 8
   ◇ A Q J 8 7
   ♣ A J 8 7 6

b. ♠ 10
   ♡ K Q 5
   ◇ A J 9 5 4
   ♣ K 10 5 3

c. ♠ A Q 4
   ♡ 6
   ◇ A K 9 8 6
   ♣ Q 9 7 6

d. ♠ Q 5
   ♡ A Q
   ◇ A Q 7 5 4
   ♣ Q 5 3 2

e. ♠ 10 8 7
   ♡ 5
   ◇ A Q 7 5 4
   ♣ A K 7 4

f. ♠ J
   ♡ 9 6
   ◇ A K 10 7 5 2
   ♣ K J 6 4

Answers on page 187

11 *Opening Two Bids*

Our hoard is little, but our hearts are great.
Alfred, Lord Tennyson

The opening bids at the one level that we have considered so far have all been non-forcing; responder is expected to pass with less than six points. But what happens if you have such a strong hand that you do not want to risk partner passing? The answer is that you open at the two level, which in principle shows at least twenty points. Let us consider the different bids in descending order.

— *TWO BIDS ARE STRONG* —

Two No-Trumps

To open two no-trumps shows a balanced hand, just like the one no-trump opener, but with 20-22 high-card points. Any of these hands would be opened with two no-trumps.

a. ♠ K J 8	b. ♠ A Q 5 4	c. ♠ K 8
♡ K J 6	♡ Q 8 6	♡ A K 6
◇ K J 4	◇ A K J 9	◇ Q 10 9
♣ A K Q 8	♣ K Q	♣ A K Q 8 7

What do you do opposite that if you are the responder? Well, you add your points to your partner's and get an immediate idea of whether you should be playing in a partscore, game or slam.

You should raise to three no-trumps if you have a balanced hand with no interest in the majors and about four to ten points.

If you have a five-card or longer spade, heart or diamond suit and at least enough points for game, bid your suit at the three level. These bids are *not* weakness take-outs. (Because the bidding has started a level higher and it is more important to be able to bid the correct game, you must forego the luxury of a weakness take-out over two no-trump openers.) In response to three of a major, the opener bids three no-trumps with only a doubleton in the bid suit, or raises the bid suit with at least three-card support.

If the responder's bid was three diamonds the opener suggests whether or not his hand is suitable for play in diamonds. If it is not, even if he has three diamonds, he bids three no-trumps. However, if he does like diamonds, he either raises or bids a four-card major-suit. (To introduce the diamond suit the responder must be able to visualise at least five diamonds as a viable contract otherwise he should just raise to three no-trumps and forget about the minor suit.)

Now let us suppose that the responder would like to investigate a possible four-four fit in a major. Yes, you guessed — he bids *three clubs, Stayman*. The opener replies:

3◇: No four-card major
3♡: Four hearts and maybe four spades
3♠: Four spades but not four hearts.

You should notice the marked similarity between this Stayman and the one over a one no-trump opening bid.

If the opener bids three diamonds, the responder can then bid three of a major to show that he has five cards in that major and four cards in the other one. (With only one five-card major the responder would bid three of that suit, not three clubs. And with no five-card major, once he has discovered that he does not have a four-four fit, he should bid the relevant number of no-trumps depending upon his point-count.)

If the opener bids three hearts and the responder would like to investigate the possibility of a four-four spade fit, he can either bid three no-trumps (the same way that the responder rebid two or three no-trumps after 1NT-2♣-2♡), or, if he has so many points that he is looking for a slam and cannot risk three no-trumps being passed, three spades. This shows specifically four spades and asks the opener either to bid three no-trumps without four spades, or four spades with the four-card holding.

The other hand type that starts with three clubs, Stayman, is one with a long club suit that is willing to bid beyond three no-trumps. In that case the responder bids three clubs, and then four clubs over whatever the opener rebids.

What about bids at the four level? Four clubs will be considered in Chapter 13. Four diamonds does not have a use because you respond three diamonds with diamonds. However, you can bid four of a major. This shows at least a six-card suit and enough points for game but no more. For example, if you pick up
♠ K J 9 7 6 4 ♡ 6 ◇ 6 5 4 ♣ 7 5 4 and partner opens two no-trumps, what contract would you like to play in? You know of at least an eight-card spade fit and a combined total of 26-28 points, counting two distributional points for your long spade suit. Just go straight to four spades.

Now what about a raise to four no-trumps? That is identical to the raise of one no-trump to four no-trumps which hopefully you will remember asks partner to go on to a slam with a maximum, but otherwise to pass. For example, raise two no-trumps to four no-trumps with something like ♠ K J 6 ♡ Q 6 4 ◇ K 6 4 2 ♣ Q 10 8, eleven high-card points. With twelve or more points and a balanced hand, take a shot at six no-trumps. A slam — what a pity your partner will be playing it rather than you!

Now for a revision test; what do you respond to a two no-trump opener holding these hands?

a. ♠ K J 7 6
   ♡ J 8 7 6
   ◇ 5
   ♣ K 7 6 3

b. ♠ K J 7 5 4
   ♡ 7 5 4
   ◇ Q 4 2
   ♣ 9 5

c. ♠ J 7
   ♡ Q 9 7
   ◇ K J 5 3
   ♣ J 8 6 3

d. ♠ 6 5 3
   ♡ 8 6 5 4 3
   ◇ 10 9 7
   ♣ 10 6

e. ♠ K 6 4
   ♡ 4 3 2
   ◇ K Q 6 4
   ♣ K 9 4

f. ♠ 6
   ♡ K 9 7 6 4 3 2
   ◇ 8 6
   ♣ 4 3 2

g. ♠ K 8
   ♡ 8 5 4
   ◇ Q 10 8 6 5 4
   ♣ 7 4

h. ♠ K J 6
   ♡ 9 7
   ◇ A 3
   ♣ K 10 7
      6 4 3

Holding *a* you would like to know if the opener has a four-card major, so respond three clubs, Stayman. If he bids three hearts or three spades, raise to game. But if he essays three diamonds, correct to three no-trumps.

Hand *b* should respond with three spades. Six high-card points and one length point are easily enough for game, and it is always best to investigate the possibility of a five-three or five-four major-suit fit. Over three spades the opener will bid three no-trumps with only a doubleton spade, but will raise to four spades with three or four spades.

Hand *c* contains eight points, all in high-cards. This gives a combined count of 28-30. Not enough for a slam but ample for game, so raise to three no-trumps.

Hand *d* in contrast must pass two no-trumps and pray that partner can bring home eight tricks. Admittedly it is unlikely, but you never know, the sun might be shining.

With hand *e* you should raise to four no-trumps. This bid shows a balanced eleven points with no interest in the majors and asks partner to go on to a slam with a maximum: either a 'good' 21 or 22 points.

Which bid did you make with *f*? I hope it was four hearts. You know about a combined holding of at least nine trumps, you have six points counting the length in hearts, and so game should be makable without too much trouble.

Hand *g* is a little tougher. It looks right to start with three diamonds, but you have only seven points counting the length in diamonds. Add this to partner's values and you have a *maximum* of 29. This means that five diamonds will probably be too high. The correct bid is three no-trumps. Your diamond suit should be a good source of tricks, and the king of spades will probably be an entry if it is needed. You should be reasonably confident that partner can bring home nine tricks (at least) in no-trumps. Of course, if you switched round the red suits then it would be correct to jump to four hearts because you usually need only 26 points to make ten tricks in a major.

Hand *h*, though, is different. Here you have thirteen total points and a slam should be on. When getting towards the six level it is imperative to try to play in the right denomination, so bid three clubs and then rebid four clubs over whatever your partner responds. He will know you have a good hand with at least five, and usually six, clubs. *If he does not like clubs he signs-off by bidding four no-trumps.*

Two Spades, Two Hearts and Two Diamonds

Now let us look at three of the suit openings. In principle the bidding is similar to that after a one-level opening bid, but this two-level opener guarantees at least a *five*-card suit and is forcing for one round – in other words the responder is not allowed to pass however bad his hand. If he has a real dog, as it is sometimes called (my average hand, you realise), then he responds two no-trumps, which is conventionally agreed as the *negative response* showing very few or no points. *If that happens and the opener rebids his own suit, the responder can pass.* He knows that the opener has eight or nine tricks in his own hand and if he really cannot see any more, he should pass. However, if the opener bids a new suit after the two no-trump negative, it is forcing; again the responder must not pass.

Let us look at an example. Suppose you pick up
♠ A K Q 6 5 ♡ A K Q 6 5 ◇ A 4 ♣ 2. Not a bad hand, is it? With friendly breaks you could make eleven tricks in your own hand, but you would like to know which major your partner prefers. So open with two spades, the higher-ranking of the two five-card suits. If (when?) partner bids the negative two no-trumps, you rebid three hearts. As this is a new suit your partner is not allowed to pass. Whatever he bids, you next go four hearts and he will know that you are at least five-five in the majors and have enough tricks for game all on your own. If he holds ♠ 7 3 2 ♡ 7 3 2 ◇ 7 3 2 ♣ 7 6 5 3 (hello again!) you will make at least ten tricks in either major unless you are very unlucky.

What happens if the responder has some values, eight or nine points, and his partner starts with an *Acol Two Bid*, as these openings are called?

If the responder has at least three-card support for the opened suit, he should raise. (It is important to realise that if the responder has very few or no points he *must* give the negative response of two no-trumps first before showing his own suit or supporting the opener. Any immediate bid other than the negative usually shows at least eight, or a good seven, points.) *A single raise promises at least one ace*; whereas *a double raise shows* support and high-card values for game but *no ace*.

If not offering support for the opener's suit, the responder can bid his own five-card or longer suit. Finally, if he has a balanced nine points or so with no five-card suit and no support for partner's suit, he can respond three no-trumps.

Have a go at these hands to check you have the idea. What should you respond if partner has opened two hearts and you hold any of the following?

i. ♠ 9 8 7 4	j. ♠ K 7	k. ♠ K 7 6 5 4	l. ♠ K 7 6 5 4
♡ 8 5 4	♡ A 7 5	♡ 6	♡ 7 5
◇ 9 6 5 4 2	◇ Q 10 7 5	◇ K J 7 5	◇ 10 7 5 4
♣ 6	♣ J 7 4 3	♣ K 9 5	♣ 9 6
m. ♠ K 7 6	n. ♠ K J 6	o. ♠ 9 8	p. ♠ K Q 8
♡ Q 10 7 6	♡ J 6	♡ 9 7 5 4 3	♡ 8 6
◇ K 7 5	◇ Q 10 8 6	◇ 9 7 6	◇ 8 5
♣ Q 9 3	♣ Q 9 6 3	♣ 9 7 6	♣ A J 9 7 6 3

Hand *i* really is becoming rather familiar — well, that number of high-card points is anyway. You must give the negative response of two no-trumps. If partner rebids three hearts you can raise to four hearts and hope that your three trumps and singleton club can produce the tenth trick. Remember that he has said that he is willing to play in three hearts even if you have one or none of them. The club shortage will allow him to ruff a loser or two in your hand to produce the extra trick(s) he needs.

Hand *j* has three-card support for a known five-card or longer suit; it also shows values and an ace, so the correct response is three hearts.

Hand *k* has more than the eight points needed to make a positive response and it has a five-card suit, so bid two spades. (This is another difference between the auctions after one-level and two-level opening bids. At the one level you are allowed, even encouraged, to respond in a four-card suit. However, at the two level it is to be avoided if at all possible. Only bid five-card suits on the first round of the auction.)

There is a similarity between hands *k* and *l*, but this one does not have enough points to make a positive response. You must respond two no-trumps and show your spades on the next round.

Hand *m* contains good heart support, values to make a positive response, but no ace. This means that the correct bid is *four* hearts.

Hand *n* is an ideal three no-trump response, showing positive values, a doubleton heart and a balanced hand.

Hand *o*: you have five hearts and yet partner opens two hearts; what could be better? But before you rush to support the hearts you must start with the negative response because you do not have enough points to bid anything else on the first round. Then you can think about supporting the hearts. (Some of my average hands are slightly better than others, you can see.)

The last hand should respond three clubs. You have enough points and a good suit of your own which partner might be able to support.

Two Clubs

This opening bid does not necessarily show clubs – it is another one of those conventional bids which has a special meaning. It shows either a balanced hand with 23 or more points, or a hand that can guarantee game all on its own. (Just in case you are not sure: to open with an Acol Two Bid is not absolutely forcing to game. As I said, if the responder gives the negative and the opener rebids his suit at the three level, the responder is allowed to pass. However, the opener can start with an Acol Two Bid on a hand that does wish to bid game because a new suit will always be forcing. The guideline to use: when you wish to play in game open an Acol Two Bid if you have two five-card or longer suits. If you only have one suit, or two suits with one of them only four cards in length, start with two clubs.)

The responses to two clubs are similar to those opposite the Acol Two Bid, except that the *negative response is two diamonds*, not two no-trumps. Of course this negative response says nothing about diamonds, it just tells the opener that the responder has less points than are needed for a positive response. All other responses are positive, showing at least eight points, or a good seven. To bid a suit shows in principle at least five, and two no-trumps promises a balanced hand. With a diamond suit, of course, you must jump to *three* diamonds as two diamonds is not natural, just the negative response.

How does the opener rebid? Let us start by considering the unbalanced hands. He just bids his suit or suits in natural sequence. He shows his longest suit first and his second suit, if he has one, on the next round.

Remember if you are the responder that you must keep the bidding open until at least game has been reached. (If you as the responder really have a bad hand, bid the minimum number of no-trumps on the second round if you cannot support partner's suit.) The bidding just follows all the principles I have expounded about one level opening bids and responses, the only difference being that game must be reached.

Now let us go on to the balanced hands. If the opener has 23-25 points he rebids two no-trumps. If the responder has at most one jack he is allowed to pass because he knows the values for game are not there. *The auction 2♣-2◇-2NT is the only one that is not forcing to game after a two club opening bid.*

If the opener has a good 25-27 points, he rebids three no-trumps. With the very unlikely 28-30 points, he rebids four no-trumps; and with 31-32 points he rebids five no-trumps. (If you find out that you are the type of person who is always picking up hands with 30 high-card points, do not play against me!)

What does the responder do when the opener has rebid two no-trumps? He bids exactly as if the opening bid had been two no-trumps. Three clubs is Stayman, and other suit bids show at least five cards.

If the opener has rebid three no-trumps then four clubs becomes Stayman, four diamonds is natural and forcing, and all higher bids are to play, the responder judging that the contract he has bid to be better than three no-trumps.

Let us look at a few examples to try to see how these bids work. What are the correct opening bids with the hands at the top of the next page?

q. ♠ A K Q 10 9   r. ♠ K J 8 6   s. ♠ A   t. ♠ K J 7
   ♡ K Q J 10 9   ♡ A Q 6   ♡ A K J 10 9 8 7   ♡ A 6
   ◇ 6 5   ◇ K 10 7   ◇ A Q 6   ◇ A Q J 9 8 7
   ♣ A   ♣ A Q J   ♣ A Q   ♣ A 6

u. ♠ A K   v. ♠ A Q J   w. ♠ K Q J 10 5 4   x. ♠ K Q J 8
   ♡ K Q J 10 9 8   ♡ K Q 8 5   ♡ A Q 4   ♡ A 6
   ◇ A Q   ◇ A K J 7   ◇ K 7   ◇ A K Q J 9 7
   ♣ 9 7 6   ♣ A 4   ♣ J 8   ♣ A

The first will want to play in game, but as it contains two five-card suits, open two spades, not two clubs.

Hand *r* has twenty points and is balanced, so the correct opening bid is two no-trumps.

Hand *s* is enormous. Clearly you want to play in at least four hearts, and if partner can produce a minor-suit king or two, you will be able to bid a slam. Start with the biggest bid you can: two clubs. Then just bid those hearts while partner tells you if he has some values.

Collection *t* is also pretty good, so open two diamonds. You cannot underwrite game, and if partner gives the negative response of two no-trumps, rebid three diamonds. If he passes that you are probably high enough.

Hand *u* has five heart tricks, two spade tricks and one top diamond trick: eight tricks, so you should open two hearts and rebid three hearts. If partner has some help he will go on to four hearts (say hand *i* given earlier).

There are 24 points in hand *v*. That means you should open two clubs and rebid two no-trumps. (Of course if partner gives the positive response of three clubs, showing eight or more points and five or more clubs, you will have to rebid three no-trumps, but he will know that you have a balanced 23-25 points.)

Hand *w* is included just to check you are still awake. It has only sixteen high-card points and two for the long spades so you must open *one* spade, not two. I hope I did not catch you out.

Finally hand *x*. This hand has only two losers: the ace of spades and the small heart. That means you can make five diamonds all on your own — or four spades if partner has four or more small cards in spades. As the second suit is only four cards in length, open two clubs.

And to end this section, what do you respond to a two club opening bid with these hands?

A. ♠ 6 5
   ♡ 9 7 5 3 2
   ◇ 8 6 5
   ♣ 5 3 2

B. ♠ K 8
   ♡ K J 7 5 4
   ◇ K 5
   ♣ 8 7 5 4

C. ♠ Q 9 7
   ♡ 8
   ◇ 9 7 5
   ♣ A J 10 6 4 2

D. ♠ Q 9 7
   ♡ J 7 5
   ◇ Q 10 6 4
   ♣ Q J 7

E. ♠ K J
   ♡ J 7
   ◇ A Q 7 5 4 3
   ♣ 10 7 5

F. ♠ Q J 9 7
   ♡ Q 10 7
   ◇ K J 8
   ♣ Q 10 5

G. ♠ Q 9 7 6 5
   ♡ 8 7 6 5 4
   ◇ 8 6
   ♣ 6

H. ♠ K J 10 6 5
   ♡ K J 10 6 5
   ◇ K 9
   ♣ 5

Hand *A* – I can just hear you saying, 'Oh no! Not again!' At least if you get cards like these in your hands at the table you will know what to bid! Yes, two diamonds, the negative response, is correct.

Hand *B* contains enough points to give a positive response and has a respectable five-card suit, so bid two hearts.

Hand *C* is also worth a positive response, and to show the club suit you must bid three clubs.

Hand *D* is a balanced eight-count, so it is worth a positive response: bid two no-trumps.

Did you bid two diamonds with *E*? I hope not. Remember that that is the negative response and that you must jump to three diamonds to show a positive with diamonds.

Hand *F* is another balanced hand, this time with eleven points. Obviously it is quite likely that you can make a slam with this hand, but start off slowly by responding two no-trumps. You can find out what type of hand partner has got and then subsequently judge what to do.

Hand *G* looks promising, especially if partner has a fit for one or other of your majors, but the point-count is too low to give an immediate positive. Start off with two diamonds and then show your majors in the later rounds of bidding.

Hand *H* is worth a positive response, and as with all auctions when you are showing your suits, start with the higher-ranking of two five-carders: two spades. Bid three hearts next time and four hearts after that to show the five-five.

I hope that gives you the idea of how the bidding develops when either you or your partner holds a big hand. Obviously that will not happen too often as twenty points is twice the average number you can expect in any one deal. But when they do arise it helps if you can bid accurately. Try the quiz to double-check that you are *au fait* with the bidding.

QUIZ

1. What opening bid would you make with these hands?

a. ♠ K Q J 7 6   b. ♠ K J 8 7   c. ♠ A K J 9 8 7 6 d. ♠ A Q 8
   ♡ A Q J 10 9   ♡ A Q   ♡ A 6   ♡ K J 8 7
   ◊ A K   ◊ K Q J 10 7 6 ◊ A K   ◊ A K Q J
   ♣ A   ♣ A   ♣ A 7   ♣ K Q

2. What do you respond if your partner opens (i) two no-trumps, (ii) two spades or (iii) two clubs when holding the following hands?

a. ♠ K J 8 7 6 b. ♠ 7 6   c. ♠ 10 7 6 5 d. ♠ A 6
   ♡ 9 6 5   ♡ A K 8 6 4 3 ♡ 9 7 6 5   ♡ 9 8 6
   ◊ 6 5 4   ◊ K 6 4   ◊ 6 5 4 3 2 ◊ 8 6
   ♣ 3 2   ♣ 10 8   ♣ None   ♣ A J 9 7 5 4

3. You open two spades and your partner responds two no-trumps; what do you rebid with these hands?

a. ♠ A Q J 9 8 7 b. ♠ A K Q 6 5 c. ♠ A K Q J 8 6 d. ♠ K 9 7 6 5
   ♡ K 7 6   ♡ K J 10 8 7   ♡ A 5   ♡ K 8 7
   ◊ A Q   ◊ A   ◊ A K   ◊ A Q 5
   ♣ A 5   ♣ K 4   ♣ 8 6 5   ♣ 10 9

4. Your partner opens two spades, you respond with the negative, two no-trumps, and he rebids three clubs. What do you bid with these hands?

a. ♠ J 8 7 6   b. ♠ 6 5   c. ♠ Q 6 4   d. ♠ 8
   ♡ 9 7   ♡ 6 4 3   ♡ 8 5 4   ♡ K 8 6 5
   ◊ K 6 5 4 3 ◊ J 9 7 6 5 ◊ 9 6 5 3 2 ◊ J 9 7 6
   ♣ 6 4   ♣ 8 4 3   ♣ 6 4   ♣ Q 8 6 5

5. Your partner opens two clubs, you respond two diamonds, negative, and he rebids (i) two spades, (ii) two no-trumps; what do you rebid with these hands?

a. ♠ K J 6   b. ♠ 6 4   c. ♠ 8 6   d. ♠ 7
   ♡ 9 7   ♡ 9 7 6 5   ♡ K 4 3 2   ♡ J 8 7 6 5 4
   ◊ Q 10 6 5 ◊ 5 3   ◊ K J 7 6 4 ◊ 7 6
   ♣ 9 6 5 4   ♣ 8 6 4 3 2 ♣ 4 3   ♣ K 8 6 5

Answers on page 187

12 *Opening Three Bids and Four Bids*

'Goodness, what beautiful diamonds.'
Lines spoken by *Mae West*

If one-level opening bids show about 13-19 points and two-level openers indicate 20 or more, what does one need to open at the three or four level? The answer is that these are weak, *pre-emptive* opening bids. They show hands not worth an opening bid at the one level but because they have a long suit they have a reasonable number of *playing tricks*. The idea behind them is to make life difficult for the opposition by taking all the bidding space away. At the same time, if you catch partner with a strong hand, as you have described yours quite accurately, he should be able to judge what to do.

To open with three or four of a suit you must have at least a *seven-card suit*. And how many tricks you promise depends on the level and the vulnerability. You should try to stay within the *Rule of Three or Five*. This means that when the opposition is non-vulnerable you should not concede more than a 300 penalty if they double and your partner has no tricks to help you out. If they are vulnerable you must not be conceding more than 500.

Where do these figures come from, and what does that imply about the number of playing tricks you are showing by the various opening bids at the three and four level?

The penalty figures of 300 and 500 come from the value of a game bid and made by the opposition. It is considered that a non-vulnerable game is worth around 400 points, so 300 is less than that; and if you have opened with a weak bid and your partner has a bad hand too, you can be pretty sure that they can make at least game.

The vulnerable game is felt to be worth around 600, so a penalty of 500 is 'good business'.

If you open with three of a suit non-vulnerable and they are non-vulnerable too, you should be hoping to make seven tricks. If they are vulnerable you need only have your sights set on six tricks. To open at the four level obviously you need one more playing trick than when you open at the three level.

— RULE OF 3 OR 5 —

Here is a classic example of a three spade opening bid at love all: ♠ K Q 10 9 8 7 6 3 ♡ 3 ◇ 5 3 ♣ 4 3. You should make seven spade tricks, and what more do you want?

You will soon discover your suit will not normally be quite as strong as that — open these bids when you think you can make a nuisance of yourself without too much risk.

There is only one other rule with these bids: do not open a three or four bid when you have four or more cards in an outside major. There is too great a risk that you will miss a good fit in that major if you do it.

Let us have a quick quiz to get the idea. Assuming that the opposition is vulnerable and that we are not (the ideal situation for a pre-empt), what would you open first in hand (i.e. you are the dealer) with these cards?

a. ♠ Q J 10 9 7 6 5
   ♡ 8
   ◇ K 8
   ♣ 5 3 2

b. ♠ J 8 7 5
   ♡ K Q 10 9 6 5 4
   ◇ 5 4
   ♣ None

c. ♠ 5
   ♡ 6
   ◇ 7 5 4
   ♣ K J 10 7 6 5 4 3

d. ♠ 8 6
   ♡ 9 8
   ◇ A Q J 10 8 6 5 4
   ♣ 7

Hand *a* is a reasonable three spade bid, though near to the minimum permitted holding.

Hand *b* should be passed because you have a side four-card major. If you open three hearts your partner will not expect that and you might miss a four spade contract. The ideal when you open a pre-empt in one major is to be very short in the other one, as in hand *a*.

You can be confident of making six tricks out of that club suit, so open three clubs with hand *c*.

Hand *d* has seven playing tricks in the diamond suit, so open four diamonds.

Note that with all these hands it helps if you do not have too many defensive tricks on the side so that if the opposition do get into the bidding, your partner will be able to judge how many tricks you can hope to take against their contract.

What do you do if your partner opens with a three bid and the next player passes? Basically you add your tricks to those that he has shown and try to assess the correct contract. For example, if he has opened three hearts at love all he has indicated seven tricks. If you can see only one or two winners, pass. However, if you think you have three or four for him, raise to four hearts.

If you have your own strong suit and a good hand you can bid your suit. This bid, if below the level of game, is forcing for one round: your partner must not pass.

The final possibility is a tactical bid. If you have such a bad hand that you can be sure the opposition can make a game, you might raise your partner's suit without any expectation of success just to make life more difficult for the fourth person as you know he will have a big hand with lots of points.

Three No-Trump Opening Bid

There is one other unusual opening bid to be covered, and that is three no-trumps. It is traditional that this opening bid shows a solid seven- or eight-card minor and no side ace or king or void; for example, ♠ 4 3 ♡ 6 4 ◇ A K Q J 10 7 6 ♣ J 7. Partner looks at his hand and decides whether or not you can make nine tricks in no-trumps. If he thinks you can because he has tricks in the other suits, he passes. However, if he thinks that the opposition will be able to beat the contract, he should bid four clubs. If that is your suit, you pass. However, if you had the above hand you would correct to four diamonds.

It is possible your partner will think you can make game in your minor but not in three no-trumps. Then he should jump to five clubs (or five diamonds if he is sure it is your suit because he has honours in clubs) and you will pass or correct to five diamonds with diamonds.

Defence to Pre-empts

You open with a pre-empt in order to make life difficult for the opposition. Naturally from time to time they will use the same tactics against you, and so it helps to have some idea of how to combat these high-level opening bids. Unfortunately though, experts still disagree as to the best defensive policy. I have recommended at the end of Chapter 16 that you use the simplest method available (the one used by many top players in Britain and by all American experts, so it must also be one of the best defences), but you will need to read the whole of that chapter first.

QUIZ

1. What opening bid would you make with these hands at game all?

a. ♠ K Q 10 7 6 5 4 3
  ♡ 8
  ◇ 8 6
  ♣ 8 5

b. ♠ 9 7 5 4
  ♡ 7
  ◇ K Q J 9 7 6 4 3
  ♣ None

c. ♠ 7 6
  ♡ 7 5
  ◇ 7 6
  ♣ Q J 10 7 6 5 4

d. ♠ J 8
  ♡ J 9
  ◇ A K Q J 10 7 6 4
  ♣ 6

2. Your partner opens three hearts at love all; what do you bid after the next person passes?

a. ♠ 8 6 5
  ♡ K 8 7
  ◇ A 5 4 2
  ♣ Q 8 7

b. ♠ 4
  ♡ Q 10 8 7
  ◇ 6 4 3 2
  ♣ J 7 5 4

c. ♠ A K J 10 7 6 5
  ♡ 6
  ◇ K J 6
  ♣ A 3

d. ♠ None
  ♡ K J 8
  ◇ A K Q 7 6
  ♣ A Q 10 7 6

3. Your partner opens three no-trumps, the next player passes, and you have to decide what to bid with these hands.

a. ♠ A 6 5
  ♡ A 6 5
  ◇ J 10 9 8 5
  ♣ 8 4

b. ♠ A K J
  ♡ 4 3
  ◇ J 9 8 7 6
  ♣ 8 5 4

c. ♠ None
  ♡ 7
  ◇ A K J 10 9 7 6 5
  ♣ 8 6 4 2

d. ♠ 7 6
  ♡ 9 7 6 5
  ◇ 9 8 6 5 4
  ♣ 5 4

Answers on page 188

13   *Slam Bidding*

Cupid and my Campaspe play'd
At cards for kisses, Cupid paid.

John Lyly

When you know that you and your partner have the approximate values
for a slam, how do you try to bid it, confident that it will make? There
are some conventions that will give you some help, but the first thing
to decide before heading towards a slam is this: *if you had one ace less
in your hand, would you still be confident that a game contract would
be impregnable*? If you would, then it is right for you to make a move
towards a slam.

If you are hoping to make twelve tricks it is obvious that the opposition must not hold two aces that they can cash. But how can you be
sure how many aces your partner holds without using illegal signals?
The answer is to use the *Blackwood Convention*, which was developed
many years ago by a top American player, Easley Blackwood. He
suggested that when a *suit* has been agreed, four no-trumps is never
used as a natural bid, so why not use it to check how many aces partner
holds? The responses given by the partner of the four no-trump bidder
are as follows:

5♣: no ace or all four aces (one assumes partner can work out which
it is!)
5◇: one ace
5♡: two aces
5♠: three aces.

Here is a simple example: you open two spades holding
♠ K Q J 10 9 ♡ A K Q J 10 ◇ K Q ♣ A, and your partner raises to
three spades. What do you think of your chances of making a slam?
You know that your partner has at least one ace for his single raise to
three spades, so you must be able to make six spades, but what about
seven? Bid four no-trumps! If he responds five diamonds, showing one

— BLACKWOOD FOR ACES —

ace, settle for six spades; but if he does reply five hearts, indicating two aces, bid seven no-trumps because you know that you have thirteen top tricks.

If, after checking on his aces, you want to know how many kings he has, then follow his response to your four no-trump bid with five no-trumps, Blackwood asking for kings. He must reply on the same lines:

6♣: no king or all four kings
6♢: one king
6♡: two kings
6♠: three kings.

(No, six no-trumps does not ask for queens because you might want to play in that contract even though a suit has been agreed — your bid of seven no-trumps on the above hand highlights that.)

But what if the opening bid was one no-trump or two no-trumps, no suit is agreed, and you want to ask for aces? Then you use the *Gerber Convention*. You jump over the no-trump bid to *four clubs*, which asks for aces. The responses are like those to Blackwood:

4♢: no ace or all four aces
4♡: one ace
4♠: two aces
4NT: three aces.

If you wish to follow this with a request for kings, bid five clubs, over which you can probably guess the responses:

5♢: no king or all four kings
5♡: one king
5♠: two kings
5NT: three kings.

When considering using Blackwood or Gerber there are three important rules to bear in mind:
(i) never bid Blackwood (or Gerber) with two losers in an unbid suit unless you are certain partner holds either the ace or king (or a singleton if proposing to play in a suit contract)
(ii) never use Blackwood (or Gerber) with a void in your hand
(iii) never ask for kings unless you know you have all the aces.

I will exhibit the reasoning behind (i) and (ii) now. Suppose you hold ♠ K Q J 10 9 ♡ A K Q J 10 ◇ 7 6 ♣ A; you open two spades and partner bids three spades. If you use Blackwood and partner admits to holding one ace, what will you do? If you bid six spades you might find he holds ♠ A 7 6 4 ♡ 7 5 4 ◇ 9 8 5 ♣ K Q 6, and he will not be amused when the opposition take the first two tricks with the ace and king of diamonds. But if you sign off in five spades he might put down in the dummy ♠ A 7 6 4 ♡ 7 5 4 ◇ K Q 5 ♣ 9 8 7 and six spades will be unbeatable. How do you find out which hand he has? You read the section just coming up on *cue-bids*.

The argument against using Blackwood with a void is similar. If you hold ♠ K Q J 10 9 ♡ A K Q J 10 ◇ K Q J ♣ None, open two spades, hear partner raise to three spades and trot out four no-trumps, Blackwood, what do you do when he shows two aces? He might have the aces of spades and diamonds, in which case you will make seven spades, or he might have the ace of clubs, in which case you will only be able to take twelve tricks. The answer? Read on!

Cue-Bids
When a suit has been agreed in a forcing auction, new suits at the four level are cue-bids. These are bids which do not necessarily promise length in a suit, but are used to show, usually, a first-round control in the suit (the ace or a void). But it is possible on occasions to show a second-round control if you are cue-bidding the same suit for a second time, bidding it at the five level. Look at the hand from above:

♠ K Q J 10 9	♠ A 7 6 4
♡ A K Q J 10	♡ 7 5 4
◇ 7 6	◇ 9 8 5
♣ A	♣ K Q 5
Opener	*Responder*
2♠	3♠
4♣	4♠
No	

Opener starts with two spades, responder supports to promise an ace, and the opener bids a new suit at the four level: a cue-bid showing first-round club control. The ball is then in the responder's court, but as he has no control in either red suit, he must bid only four spades. This tells the opener that there are two diamond losers and he can safely pass.

♠ K Q J 10 9	♠ A 7 6 4
♡ A K Q J 10	♡ 7 5 4
◇ 7 6	◇ K Q 5
♣ A	♣ 9 8 7
Opener	*Responder*
2♠	3♠
4♣	4◇
4NT	5◇
6♠	No

The first three bids are the same, but this time the responder has a control in diamonds. Admittedly he would like it to be a first-round control, but he cannot have everything. He knows that the opener can use Blackwood, just to check, after which the responder shows his ace and the opener bids six spades.

♠ K Q J 10 9	♠ A 7 6 4
♡ A K Q J 10	♡ 7 5 4
◇ 7 6	◇ A 8 5
♣ A	♣ 9 8 7
Opener	*Responder*
2♠	3♠
4♣	4◇
4NT	5♡
7♠	No

This time the responder does have a first-round diamond control, is able to show two aces over Blackwood, and the opener can bid seven spades, confident that he will throw dummy's diamond losers on his heart tricks and ruff his diamond loser in the dummy even if East does not have a king.

As an example of Gerber, suppose you pick up
♠ K 7 ♡ K Q 10 9 6 4 3 2 ◇ 6 ♣ K 5 and hear partner open two no-trumps. After recovering from the pleasant surprise, you bid four clubs, Gerber. If partner bids four diamonds to show you all four

aces, you bid seven no-trumps knowing that you have two spade, eight heart, one diamond and two club tricks. However, if he bids four no-trumps to show three aces, you jump to six hearts. And, horror of horrors, if he can only own up to two aces by bidding four spades, then you must bid five hearts and he should pass. *The man who has used Blackwood or Gerber is in control of the auction.*

QUIZ

1. In which of these auctions is the four no-trump bid Blackwood?

a. Opener	Responder	b. Opener	Responder	c. Opener	Responder
1♠	3♠	1NT	4NT	2♣	2◇
4♣	4♡			2♡	3♡
4NT				3♠	4NT

d. Opener	Responder
1♠	3♣
3♡	3NT
4◇	4NT

2. In which of these auctions is the last call a cue-bid?

a. Opener	Responder	b. Opener	Responder	c. Opener	Responder
2♣	2◇	1NT	3♠	1NT	3♠
2♡	3♡	3NT	4♣	4♣	
4♣					

d. Opener	Responder
2NT	3♣
3♡	3♠
4◇	

3. Without looking, can you remember the three rules which tell you when not to use Blackwood?

4. What does four no-trumps mean in this auction?

Opener	Responder
2♡	4♡
4NT	

Answers on page 188

14   *You Open, They Enter The Bidding*

He bored with his augur, he bored once or twice,
And some were playing cards, and some were playing
    dice.

                                Helen of Kirkconnell

So far the opposition has remained remarkably quiet while you have
been bidding all the hands. However, as you will soon find out, they
tend to prefer to get involved in the action. They did not sit down just
to pass and watch you and your partner having all the fun.

First of all we will consider what happens when you have opened
the bidding and they decide to *overcall*, that is to bid a suit or no-
trumps.

— YOU OPEN, THEY COUNTER—ATTACK —

The usual policy is that if the responder (or the opener if the responder has bid and the fourth hand has entered the bidding) thinks that the overcaller has made a mistake and that the contract is going down, he doubles. (From the section on scoring you will remember that this increases the penalties available if they do go down.) To give you a guideline, it is normally right to double them if you have a good holding in their proposed trump suit and are short in your partner's suit. If your hand is strong in their suit and you have three or more cards in your partner's suit, be wary of doubling; you might not collect as many tricks as you expect.

As an example, suppose you hold

♠ K J 9 5 4 ♡ 4 ◇ A 5 4 ♣ 10 8 6 5, your partner opens one heart and the next hand bids one spade. Do you think he is going to make it? You have three or four trump tricks, the ace of diamonds and your partner opened the bidding. You have only eight high-card points, so you might not even be able to make a game. Get in there and double!

If you cannot double when they overcall, just try to make your natural bid. However, remember that you still need nine points to bid at the two level. For example, suppose you hold

♠ K J 8 7 ♡ 5 4 ◇ 6 5 ♣ K 7 6 5 4, your partner opens one heart and you are just about to bid one spade when the next hand overcalls with two diamonds. How annoying! As you do not have the necessary number of points to bid at the two level and you do not have enough hearts to support your partner's suit, you must pass and perhaps bid later if the opportunity presents itself.

If they overcall you can only bid no-trumps with at least one stopper in their suit. So if you hold ♠ 10 8 7 ♡ J 7 ◇ K J 8 7 ♣ Q 10 6 5, your partner opens one heart and just before you can say one no-trump, the next man bids one spade, you are in an awkward position. Again you should pass and hope that they get too high.

If you have three trumps to an honour you could support your partner, just to let him know that he is not fighting alone. Normally this is not recommended in an uncontested auction, but if some in-fighting is about to begin, it helps to give your partner some idea of how many points you have. For example, if you pick up

♠ 10 8 ♡ Q 7 6 ◇ K J 5 3 ♣ Q 6 4 3, your partner opens one heart and the next hand bids one spade, you should bid two hearts. Partner will expect you to have four trumps, but you cannot have everything in this world, and rules are sometimes made to be broken. At least by bidding two hearts you tell your partner that you have 6-9 points and some heart support. He knows he is not fighting a lone battle against the two bad guys. So if they overcall, make a bid if you can, but do not do anything foolhardy.

If they overcall one no-trump, which you will see in the next chapter always shows a strong no-trump when made directly over the opening bid, there is a slight difference in bidding style. Because the overcaller is known to have a good hand, it is unlikely that you and your partner will be able to make a game. So you double with any good hand if you think they will make not one no-trump, but if you bid a suit at the two level it is *non-forcing* showing a hand too weak to double with a long suit of its own. For example, if you hold
♠ 5 4 ♡ 6 4 ◇ Q 10 8 7 6 5 4 3 ♣ 3, partner opens one heart and the next hand overcalls one no-trump, bid two diamonds. In this case the overcall has helped. If the opponent had passed, so would you have had to because you do not have the values to make a bid at the two level in diamonds. But now he has overcalled one no-trump, you can bid two diamonds without misleading your partner about your hand.

There is one rather more advanced gadget that is employed in certain auctions, which involves a bid of the opponent's suit. (If you wish, skip this bit and come back to it when you have been playing for a few months; you can get along without it.) Suppose you have picked up
♠ 5 4 3 2 ♡ J 6 4 ◇ A Q 10 ♣ A J 10, heard your partner open one heart and the next hand overcall one spade. What do you bid? You have enough points to be able to hope to make a game, but you cannot give jump support in hearts with only three, and you do not have your own suit to show. You cannot bid no-trumps because you do not have a spade stopper. What can you do? The answer is that you bid the opponent's suit: two spades. This bid cannot be natural because if you wanted to mention spades you would double for penalties, as we saw earlier in this chapter. It says that you have enough points to think that your side can make a game but that you have no bid available. Partner should bid no-trumps if he can, or make his normal rebid. Given the above hand, if your partner rebids two no-trumps over two spades, raise to three no-trumps. If he bids a minor at the three level he must have five hearts, so jump to four hearts. And finally, if he rebids three hearts, again showing at least five, raise to four hearts.

A bid of the opponent's suit like this is rather misleadingly called a *cue-bid* as no control is promised in the suit.

QUIZ

1. Your partner opens one diamond and the next hand bids one spade; what do you call with the following hands?

a. ♠ Q 10 7 6
   ♡ J 7 6 5
   ◇ Q 2
   ♣ K 7 5

b. ♠ J 7 6
   ♡ Q 10 8 7
   ◇ J 6
   ♣ 10 6 4 3

c. ♠ K 10 5 4
   ♡ A 4
   ◇ 6 4
   ♣ A J 10 7 6

d. ♠ K J 7 6
   ♡ Q 10 7
   ◇ A 10 8
   ♣ 10 7 6

e. ♠ J 7 6
   ♡ Q 10 8 7
   ◇ A 5
   ♣ K Q 10 7

f. ♠ 8 7 6
   ♡ Q 10 8 7
   ◇ K J 8
   ♣ Q 7 5

2. Your partner opens one heart and the next hand overcalls one no-trump, showing 15-17 points and at least one heart stopper. What do you bid with these hands?

a. ♠ Q 10 6 5
   ♡ 9 7
   ◇ K J 7 6
   ♣ Q 7 5

b. ♠ K J 8 6
   ♡ Q 10 7
   ◇ A 8 7
   ♣ Q 9 5

c. ♠ 8 6
   ♡ K 8 7 6
   ◇ A J 10 7
   ♣ 5 3 2

d. ♠ K J 10 7 6 5
   ♡ 4
   ◇ Q 10 8 7 6
   ♣ 5

Answers on page 189

15   *They Open, You Enter The Bidding*

Horny hands that hold the aces which this morning
held the plough.

Sir John Betjeman

Finally we get to the section on bidding after the opposition has had
the first word. If you wish to bid a suit yourself there are a few things
that you should bear in mind. You already know that your right-hand
opponent has at least thirteen points, and if his partner has some values

— THEY OPEN, YOU COUNTER—ATTACK —

as well, they might be able to double you and collect a good penalty. This means that you should exercise some discretion, but counter-attack is often the best defence. It does usually pay to get into the bidding. So you should:

(i) only overcall with at least five cards in your suit

(ii) have a strong suit that you are prepared for partner to lead

(iii) do not have most of your points in the suit bid on your right

(iv) consider the vulnerability.

You are allowed to overcall with relatively few points if you have a good suit because it will serve several purposes:

(i) you will tell partner which suit to lead should they outbid you (this will be particularly important if they end up in a no-trump contract)

(ii) overcalling will make it more difficult for them to bid to the correct contract if they should be outbidding you

(iii) the hand might belong to you, and then one of you should be getting into the bidding. If you can make a bid do not leave it to your partner, get into the action

(iv) it is possible that you will be able to make a profitable *sacrifice*.

To give you a few examples, the following hands would be considered quite acceptable to overcall a one club opener with one spade:

a. ♠ A K J 10 7   b. ♠ K J 10 8 7 6
   ♡ Q 5   ♡ K 7
   ♢ 9 7 6 4   ♢ 6 5 3
   ♣ 4 2   ♣ 4 2

The advantage of bidding one spade over one club is that you use up all the bidding space at the one level. No longer can your left-hand opponent peacefully respond one of a red suit, and if he wishes to bid two of his suit he has to go above his partner's club suit, so they will be reaching at least the three level; and his hand might not warrant bidding that high.

One would make these calls either non-vulnerable or vulnerable, but always remember to employ more discretion when vulnerable; the penalties are much larger if the weather is stormy and you go two or three down doubled.

If you are the fourth player to speak and both opponents have bid, follow the same principles but be even more careful. The opener has more idea of what to expect from the responder's hand, and he will be only too happy to collect a large penalty if you give him the chance to take it.

Jump Overcalls

What does it mean when you overcall, say, one heart with *two* spades, a jump bid? The answer is that you show at least a respectable six-card suit and six or seven playing tricks. In high-card terms this means about fifteen points. For example, you would bid two spades over one heart holding ♠ A Q J 9 7 6 ♡ K 7 ◇ K Q 4 ♣ 3 2. In fact you could bid two spades with a fraction less; but partner will assume six or seven playing tricks, a good six-card suit and will bid accordingly.

Of course all the rules governing simple overcalls apply here as well, and as you have bid one level higher than necessary, you must have that sixth trump and an extra high-card or two.

One No-Trump Overcall

If you bid one no-trump over the opening bid on your right it shows a strong no-trump with at least one stopper (preferably two) in the suit bid on your right regardless of the vulnerability. It is far too dangerous to make an immediate overcall of one no-trump with a weak no-trump because the third hand, if he has some values, will be able to double you, confident of a juicy penalty.

This would be a good one no-trump overcall after a one heart opening bid: ♠ K J 7 ♡ A Q 8 7 ◇ A Q 10 7 ♣ 10 8.

What do you do if your partner overcalls one no-trump and the next man passes? Then a cue-bid of the opponent's suit acts as Stayman, and all other two level suit bids as weakness take-outs. Other bids are as opposite a one no-trump opener.

A Bid of Their Suit

Occasionally you will have such a strong hand, even though they have opened the bidding, that you know you can make a game. If that pleasant situation ever arises, you give your partner the good news by bidding two of their suit; in other words you cue-bid directly, though note that cue-bids that are at low levels do not promise a control in the suit. For example,

West	North	East	South
1◇	2◇		

North's two diamond bid tells his partner that he can make game in his own hand and that the auction must progress until at least game has been reached. This is called a *game-forcing situation*.

Normally the cue-bidder will have either a very strong one-suiter like ♠ A K Q 10 8 7 6 5 ♡ A K 7 ◇ 6 ♣ 10, or a two-suiter like ♠ K Q J 9 8 7 ♡ A K ◇ None ♣ K Q J 10 6.

Your partner should bid his lowest suit, and then you, the cue-bidder, will either bid your one suit twice, or show your two suits, leaving it to partner to decide where to play.

In the Protective Position

If your left-hand opponent opens the bidding and the next two players pass, you are said to be in the fourth seat or in the *protective position*. Your partner might have been forced to pass over the opening bid even with a fair number of points because he had no convenient bid to make: he had no five-card or longer suit and he could not bid one no-trump, so he was fixed into passing. If this is the case, you must protect his values and get your side into the auction. It is considered reasonable to overcall on any hand that would have made an immediate overcall, and perhaps with a hand that would be not quite worth an immediate overcall. And if you bid one no-trump this shows a weak no-trump, not a strong no-trump. (In response to this protective no-trump, the cue-bid is still used as Stayman, and other suit bids at the two level are weakness take-outs.)

A jump overcall in the protective position is slightly weaker than it would be immediately over the opening bid, but it still guarantees at least a six-card suit.

A cue-bid in the fourth seat has the same meaning as in the second seat: a game-going hand.

Responding to an Overcall

If your partner has made a simple overcall, whether in the second or fourth seat, the only forcing bid you can make is to cue-bid the opponent's suit. If you bid a new suit without cue-bidding it is non-forcing, suggesting that you think this might be a better spot than the one partner has proposed. If you jump into a new suit it is also non-forcing, but it is encouraging. Partner is expected to bid on if he is suitable for play in your suit.

If you cue-bid partner is expected to describe his hand further, either by rebidding his suit to show a minimum, or by bidding no-trumps if he has a stopper or two in their suit, or by showing another suit if he has one and his hand is better than a complete minimum. Whatever the overcaller bids, if the cue-bidder introduces a new suit it is forcing. (If he did not want to force he would not cue-bid first.)

However, if partner has made a *jump* overcall, a new suit by you is forcing. The lack of bidding space necessitates this — you must bid your games accurately.

QUIZ

1. What would you overcall (i) in the second seat (ii) in the fourth seat if the dealer opens one club? (If in the fourth seat assume the partner of the dealer passes.)

a. ♠ K J 7
   ♡ 10 8 6
   ◇ K 10 6
   ♣ K Q 10 6

b. ♠ K 7
   ♡ A Q 10 7 6
   ◇ K 7 5 4
   ♣ 8 5

c. ♠ A Q J 10 7 6
   ♡ K 9 8
   ◇ 7 6
   ♣ K 6

d. ♠ A Q 10 8 7 6
   ♡ 7 6
   ◇ K Q 6
   ♣ 5 4

e. ♠ 8 7 6
   ♡ A Q 10 9 7
   ◇ 6
   ♣ J 8 7 5

f. ♠ K 8
   ♡ K J 8 6
   ◇ Q 9 7
   ♣ A Q J 8

2. The dealer opens one diamond and your partner overcalls one heart. After the next player passes, what do you bid with these hands?

a. ♠ Q J 10 8 7 6
   ♡ 6
   ◇ K 7 5
   ♣ 10 8 6

b. ♠ K 8 7 6 5
   ♡ Q 5
   ◇ 9 7 5
   ♣ J 6 4

c. ♠ 9 8 7
   ♡ J 8
   ◇ K J 8 5
   ♣ K J 8 5

d. ♠ A Q 7 6
   ♡ Q 7
   ◇ A Q 10 6
   ♣ J 8 5

e. ♠ A 8 7 5
   ♡ K 9 8 7
   ◇ K 7 5
   ♣ 6 5

f. ♠ K 9 8 7
   ♡ K 8
   ◇ Q J 10 6
   ♣ K J 8

g. ♠ A K J 10 7 6
   ♡ Q 7
   ◇ K Q 8
   ♣ A 6

h. ♠ A Q J 10 7 6
   ♡ 7
   ◇ K J 7
   ♣ Q 10 8

3. The person on your right opens one diamond, you overcall one spade, the third player passes and your partner cue-bids with two diamonds. What would you bid with each of these hands?

a. ♠ A Q 10 7 6   b. ♠ A Q J 9 8
   ♡ K 8 6   ♡ K Q 10 6
   ◊ 7 6 5   ◊ 6
   ♣ 7 6   ♣ 10 8 6

c. ♠ A Q J 9 6   d. ♠ A Q 10 8 6 5
   ♡ 10 7 6   ♡ 10 8 5
   ◊ A Q 9   ◊ 8
   ♣ J 8   ♣ K J 6

4. Your left-hand opponent opens one diamond and your partner overcalls one no-trump. When the next player passes, what do you bid with these hands?

a. ♠ K J 8   b. ♠ K J 7 6
   ♡ K J 7   ♡ Q 10 8 7
   ◊ 9 7 5   ◊ 8
   ♣ Q 10 7 6 ♣ K 7 6 4

c. ♠ K 10 6 5 d. ♠ Q 10 8 6 5 4
   ♡ 9 7 5   ♡ 8 7 6
   ◊ Q 6 4   ◊ 7 5
   ♣ J 10 3   ♣ 7 5

5. Your right-hand opponent opens one heart and it is passed round to your partner; he bids one no-trump. What do you bid with these hands after the dealer passes?

a. ♠ K J 8   b. ♠ K 10 9 7   c. ♠ Q 10 7   d. ♠ KJ875
   ♡ 10 8 6 5   ♡ 7 6 5 4   ♡ K J 7   ♡ 8
   ◊ A Q 10 7 ◊ A Q J 9   ◊ 9 7 6   ◊ Q1075
   ♣ A 5   ♣ K   ♣ A J 7 5 ♣ 8 7 6

6. Your partner has overcalled one club with two spades. What do you bid on these hands when the next player passes?

a. ♠ 9   b. ♠ K 8   c. ♠ 7 6   d. ♠ K 8
   ♡ A Q 10 8 7 6 ♡ 10 8 6   ♡ K J 10 7 6 5 ♡ A K 8 6 5
   ◊ A K 6   ◊ K J 10 5 ◊ Q 6 5   ◊ K 8 7
   ♣ 9 8 6   ♣ A Q 7 6   ♣ 9 8   ♣ 10 7 5

Answers on page 189

16   *The Take-Out Double*

There be that can pack the cards and yet cannot play
well.

Francis Bacon

There is one other invaluable device that you can use when entering
the bidding. Suppose you pick up the following hand:
♠ A Q 9 7 ♡ K J 8 7 ◇ A 10 7 6 ♣ 5, and your right-hand opponent
opens one club; what do you bid? You have easily enough points to
enter the bidding, but you do not have a five-card suit and you cannot
bid one no-trump. So what do you do? You would like your partner
to tell you which of the other three suits, excluding clubs, the suit
opened, he prefers. There is a conventional way to do that: you double.

TAKE-OUT DOUBLE

109

This is called a *take-out double*, which asks partner to tell you his longest suit and to give you some idea of how strong his hand is.

How can you tell when a double is for take-out or penalties? The answer is that if your partner has not made a positive bid (he either has not had a turn or he has passed) and it is your first turn to bid, then a double is for take-out. The double is also for take-out if you opened the bidding, your partner passed and it is your turn to speak again.

Here are some auctions when the double is for take-out.

	West	North	East	South
a.	1♡	Dble.		
b.	1◇	No	No	Dble.
c.	1♣	No	1♡	Dble.
d.		1◇	No	No
	1♡	Dble.		
e.		1◇	No	No
	2♣	Dble.		
f.		1♡	1♠	No
	No	Dble.		
g.		1♡	1♠	No
	2♠	Dble.		

When do you make a take-out double? When you have a hand that wants partner to tell you which is his best suit. In *a* or *b* above it is ideally a three-suited hand with at least twelve high-card points and shortage in the suit opened. (One usually bids with the understanding that if a hand is strong enough to open the bidding, it is strong enough to make a take-out double in these two auctions if the shape of the hand is suitable.)

However, in *c*, because the opponents have bid two suits, you are asking your partner to choose between the other two, so you should have a two-suiter, and some extra values would not go amiss as both opponents are bidding.

In *d* you should have a very strong three-suiter that has at least sixteen high-card points, preferably more. You are telling partner that you know he has less than six points because he has already passed, but that you still want to contest the auction. You should be short in the suit bid on your right, and with length in the other three suits, ideally something like ♠ A K 6 4 ♡ 7 ◇ A J 10 7 ♣ K Q J 7.

In *e* you are also asking partner to bid no matter how weak his hand, and as that will be at the two level you should have an absolute

minimum of sixteen points. The sort of hand worth this bid is
♠ K J 10 ♡ A Q 7 6 ◇ A K J 8 7 ♣ 5. (Note that in all these examples
the ideal holding in their suit is a singleton or void because then you
have length in the other three suits.)

Auctions *f* and *g* are similar, showing strong hands.

Occasionally you will have such a strong hand that you must make a
take-out double without the ideal distribution, but the extra strength
will make up for it. Suppose you hold
♠ A Q 10 ♡ 10 9 8 7 ◇ A K 10 9 ♣ A Q and they open one club
on your right. What do you do? You cannot bid one no-trump because
that shows only 15-17 points. The answer is that you double and then
bid no-trumps at the minimum level, showing a hand too strong to
overcall one no-trump directly: about 18-20 points with at least one
trick in the suit opened by the opposition.

Responding to Take-Out Doubles

The obvious point is that if you are being asked to bid your best suit,
bid it! But, of course, it is not quite as simple as that because you
should try to give your partner an idea of how many points you hold
so that he can then judge the combined values of the hands. (His take-
out double, as you have seen, can be anything from thirteen points
upwards.)

The first thing to realise is that if your partner makes a take-out
double and the next hand passes, you must bid even if you have no
high-card points at all. For example, you hold
♠ 9 8 7 5 4 ♡ 4 3 2 ◇ 5 4 3 ♣ 3 2, the person on your left opens
one club, your partner doubles and the next player passes. *You must
bid one spade.* If you pass one club it is virtually certain that they will
make it. The only time you are allowed to pass a take-out double is
when you are very strong in *their* suit and you are converting the
double to penalties. For example, in the above auction in which your
partner doubles a one club opener, if you hold
♠ 6 4 3 ♡ 3 ◇ K 5 3 ♣ K Q 10 9 8 6, it would not be unreasonable
to pass, and then sit back and collect the nice penalty from one club
doubled. However, these hands are very rare. In general you will respond
to a take-out double. (Of course, if you have no points and the partner
of the opening bidder does not pass over the take-out double, you are
off the hook and can pass, letting out an inaudible sigh!)

If you have to bid with no points, what do you do when you have got some values? The answer is that you jump in your suit if you have about 8-10 points: a hand that would make a strong single raise or a weak double raise if your partner had opened the suit you are about to bid. For example, if you have ♠ K Q 10 7 ♡ K 9 8 ◇ 10 8 7 6 ♣ 5 3, and your partner doubles one club, jump to two spades. Mentally imagine that your partner has just opened one spade; what would you bid? The answer is two spades with a bit to spare, so bid it now. Remember that your partner has supposedly got support for all the suits you might bid at this point in the auction.

If you have a balanced hand, at least one stopper in their suit and you feel you should be bidding no-trumps, you make the same bid as you would have produced if partner had opened the bidding. So one no-trump shows 6-9 points, two no-trumps 10-12 and three no-trumps 13-15. Try to have two stoppers in their suit for the last bid because you could cue-bid instead, as explained next.

What if you have even more points than ten, so you can envisage game being on?

Then you cue-bid the opponent's suit! Give yourself ♠ K Q 10 9 ♡ K Q 7 ◇ K 7 6 5 ♣ 5 4 after your partner has doubled one club for take-out. You have an opening bid, so you should be able to make a game. Give him the good news that you have a strong hand: bid two clubs, the opener's suit. After that suits are shown until a fit is found.

They Make a Take-Out Double

There is one other facet of the take-out double that we need to consider, and it really fits into Chapter 14. What happens when your partner has made an opening bid and the next opponent makes a take-out double?

If this situation arises the normal rules for bidding are altered somewhat. Suppose you hold ♠ Q J 9 7 6 4 ♡ 5 4 3 ◇ 2 ♣ Q 5 4, your partner opens one diamond and the next player doubles. If you pass, there is a risk that your left-hand opponent will also pass, converting the take-out double into one for penalties. As your hand will be remarkably useless in diamonds, it is correct for you to bid one spade. A simple bid over a take-out double shows a weak hand with a long suit, and usually implies shortage in partner's suit because you were unwilling to risk the fourth player converting the double from take-out to penalties.

If simple bids, even at the two level if made without a jump, are weak, what do you do with better hands? Well, a one no-trump bid retains its normal meaning, a balanced hand with, in this case, seven-to-nine points. And if you have four-card support for partner you can raise his suit, but you can be a little more aggressive than usual to make it more difficult for the next player to enter the bidding. For example, your partner opens one spade, the next player doubles and you hold ♠ K 9 8 7 ♡ 5 4 ◇ A J 10 6 ♣ 6 4 3; bid *three* spades! It is possible that they can make a heart contract, but the fourth player might find it difficult, if not impossible, to enter the auction at the four level. The normal values for raises are that a single raise shows 5-8 total points (counting both high-card and distributional values) and a double raise promises 9-10 total points. So what does one do with the eleven- or twelve-point hands that would have made a double raise without the intervening double? There is a gadget available, but skip over this bit unless you are absorbing all the material in this book without difficulty, or you have been playing for some time. When you have a balanced eleven or twelve points, a hand that would normally respond two no-trumps to your partner's opening bid, it is often better to try to extract a penalty from the opposition to teach them to try to enter your auctions. (How this is done I will explain in a moment.) This frees two no-trumps from its usual meaning and allows one to use it to show a *high-card raise* to the three level in partner's suit. For example, if you hold ♠ 8 6 ♡ A Q 6 5 ◇ K J 10 6 ♣ 9 6 5 and partner opens one heart, you would normally respond three hearts. But if your right-hand opponent doubles, bid two no-trumps instead to tell your partner about your high-card values. He can then sign off in three or four of the major, or make a game-try in another suit.

The corollary of this is that a double raise is a little weaker in high-cards, making it a distributional or slightly pre-emptive raise.

But what do you do with a normal two no-trump response or a strong hand that cannot risk partner passing a simple response? The answer is that you *redouble*. In principle this shows at least a good nine points and tells partner that you will make at least one more bid if he passes a call around to you.

As you are telling your partner that your side has the balance of the points, it might be possible to obtain a juicy penalty from the opposition. So if you hold four or more cards in a suit they bid and are short in partner's suit, double them. To give an ideal example, you pick up ♠ K J 8 7 ♡ Q J 7 6 ◇ A 10 9 7 ♣ 3, partner opens one club and the next player doubles: redouble, and whichever suit the next player bids, double him. You should be able to extract a penalty and you might not even have game on. (Note that the best holding is a singleton in your partner's suit so that his top cards in that suit will be worth tricks.)

If the opener has four cards in the suit bid on his right after a double and a redouble, he should double to tell his partner the good news.

A redouble can also be made on a strong hand that could not risk a simple, non-forcing response over the take-out double. For example, if you hold ♠ A Q J 8 7 ♡ 6 5 ◇ A Q 6 5 3 ♣ 3, your partner opens one heart and the next hand doubles, redouble. If they bid spades or diamonds, double them, but if they bid clubs and partner does not double, bid two spades. He will know that you have a good hand because you did not bid one spade originally. He should keep the bidding open for at least one more round.

If you have a good hand but with only one suit, make a jump shift into that suit over the double, which is forcing to game. For example, with ♠ A Q J 8 7 6 ♡ K 6 ◇ K 8 ♣ 9 8 7, over an opening bid of one of any suit other than spades and a take-out double, jump to two spades, game forcing and showing a strong one-suited hand. The bidding then continues normally.

To recap: if your partner opens the bidding and the next player doubles, a simple change of suit bid is non-forcing, showing a long suit in a weak hand. A jump shift shows a strong one-suiter and is forcing to game. Raises of partner's suit are pre-emptive in style, trying to make life more difficult for the next player to enter the bidding, and so two no-trumps is bid whenever you hold a high-card raise to the three level (11 or 12 high-card points). All other good hands redouble on the first round.

Defence to Pre-empts

The easiest way to deal with pre-empts is to use a take-out double when you would like partner to bid his best suit. All other bids, including three no-trumps, are natural. Some people call this an Optional Double, but really they mean a take-out double; as with all take-out doubles, partner can exercise the option to pass, converting it to a penalty double.

One other hint when contemplating bidding over a pre-empt: it is dangerous entering the auction at the three or four level, so assume that partner holds seven high-card points and judge whether to bid or not on that basis. To go along with this, if your partner overcalls or makes a take-out double against a pre-empt, remember that he has bid seven of your points already.

This is a difficult part of bridge — bid using your intuition! (Women occasionally find bridge much easier than men!)

QUIZ

1. Which of these hands would make a take-out double of a one diamond opening bid on your right?

a. ♠ 10 8 7 6
  ♡ A Q J 7
  ◇ 6
  ♣ 10 8 6 4

b. ♠ K J 7 6
  ♡ A Q 6 4
  ◇ 7
  ♣ K J 6 3

c. ♠ J 10 8 7
  ♡ K J 7
  ◇ A Q 5
  ♣ K Q 8

d. ♠ 8 7
  ♡ A Q J 8 6
  ◇ K 8 7
  ♣ 10 8 7

e. ♠ A K Q J 10
  ♡ A K Q J 10
  ◇ None
  ♣ 4 3 2

f. ♠ K J 7 6
  ♡ A Q 8
  ◇ A Q 10
  ♣ K J 6

2. Your left-hand opponent opens one diamond, your partner doubles and the next hand passes; what do you bid with these hands?

a. ♠ 10 8 7
  ♡ Q 7
  ◇ K Q 10 7
  ♣ J 8 6 5

b. ♠ K J 7 6
  ♡ K J 7 6
  ◇ 8 7
  ♣ A Q 6

c. ♠ 8 6 5
  ♡ K 7 6
  ◇ A Q J 10 8 7
  ♣ 6

d. ♠ K 8 6
  ♡ Q 10 7
  ◇ A Q 10
  ♣ 9 8 6 5

e. ♠ 7 6
  ♡ 8 6 5
  ◇ 8 7 3
  ♣ 8 6 5 3 2

f. ♠ K J 7
  ♡ A Q 6
  ◇ 8 6 5 4
  ♣ K J 7

g. ♠ A Q J 8 7
  ♡ K 8 7
  ◇ 7 5
  ♣ K 8 5

h. ♠ 8 6
  ♡ K J 7 6 5
  ◇ 7 5 4
  ♣ K 7 6

3. Your partner opens one diamond and the next player doubles; what do you bid with the following hands?

a. ♠ K 7
♡ K Q J 9 8 7
◇ A 4
♣ 6 4 3

b. ♠ 8 6 5
♡ 7 6
◇ K Q 6 4
♣ 8 5 4 2

c. ♠ K J 7 6
♡ A Q 6 3
◇ 7
♣ K 6 5 3

d. ♠ K J 7
♡ Q 10 7
◇ J 6 5
♣ J 8 6 5

e. ♠ K 7 6
♡ 9 7 6 5
◇ J 7 6
♣ Q 6 4

f. ♠ K Q 6 5 4
♡ A Q 7 6 4
◇ 7
♣ K 5

g. ♠ K 7
♡ 9 8 6 5
◇ K Q 10 8 7
♣ 6 4

h. ♠ K 7
♡ K J 7
◇ K J 7 6 5
♣ 7 5 3

4. Your right-hand opponent opens three diamonds; what do you bid with these hands?

a. ♠ A K J 10 7 5
♡ A Q 4
◇ 7 3
♣ 7 3

b. ♠ K Q 10 9
♡ A J 8 7
◇ 4
♣ K J 7 6

c. ♠ A Q 7
♡ K J 8
◇ A Q 7
♣ K J 5 4

d. ♠ 10 8 5
♡ A K 6
◇ KJ982
♣ 7 5

5. Your left-hand opponent opens three clubs, your partner doubles for take-out and the next player passes; what do you bid with these hands?

a. ♠ A Q J 6
♡ 8 4 3
◇ 8 4 3
♣ 8 4 3

b. ♠ 7 5
♡ A K J 8 4
◇ 7 6 4 2
♣ A 8

c. ♠ 7 5
♡ K J 3
◇ 109765
♣ A Q 6

d. ♠ 4
♡ 5 3
◇ 98653
♣ KQ987

Answers on page 190

Section B

The Play of the Cards

I   No-Trump Contracts

17   *Suit Combinations*

The accursed power which stands on Privilege
(And goes with Women, and Champagne, and Bridge)
Broke — and Democracy resumed her reign;
(Which goes with Bridge, and Women and Champagne).
Hilaire Belloc

Now we get on to the second stage of bridge: the play of the cards.
The auction has finished and one of the four players is about to be the
declarer in a contract. The opening lead is made, declarer's partner puts
down his dummy and suddenly everyone can see 26 cards, not just his
own thirteen.

Let us turn to the declarer. The first thing to do when the dummy
appears is to *stop and think*. Even if there is a singleton in the dummy
in the suit led, do not play it immediately. There are more contracts
lost by insufficient thought and preparation at trick one than at any
other. You should spend as long as you need planning how you will
play out the hand. Check your line of play, look for snags, see where
you have tricks, see where others can come from.

*In all deals South, the bottom hand, will be the declarer and North
the dummy.*

I will start by considering no-trump contracts because in some ways
they are easier to analyse than suit contracts. When the dummy comes
down, forget the auction, even if you think your partner has bid badly;
just concentrate on making your contract.

When playing in a no-trump contract, start by counting your top
tricks: those you could take by just leading out all your winners. Of
course if that total is equal to or greater than the number you said you
would make, there is nothing to worry about. But usually things will
not be so simple.

Let us start by considering this 'top tricks' business. How many are
there in this combination? (We will ignore the other suits for the
moment.)

119

K 8 7

A Q 5

The correct answer is *three*. You can take one trick with the ace, one with the king and the third with the queen. That might not seem too difficult. What about this suit?

A J 9 7

K 6 4 2

This time the answer is only *two*: the ace and the king must win tricks. Clearly, if the queen falls under either the ace or king, then you will be able to cash the jack too. But you must start by assuming only two top tricks.

Another one:

Q 8 6 5

A 7 4

This time there is only one top trick: the ace.

K 8 7

Q J 10 6

Now there is none: you do not have the ace, so you do not have a top trick.

So start by counting your top tricks. Here is a complete hand; how many top tricks do you have counting all four suits?

♠ A 7 5 4
♡ Q 10 8
◇ J 7
♣ K Q J 6

♠ K 7
♡ K 7 5 4 3
◇ A K 8
♣ A 7 5

In spades you have the ace and king: two top tricks. In hearts you do not have the ace, so there are no top tricks. In diamonds the ace and king produce two top tricks. And in clubs you can cash the ace, king, queen and jack: four more top tricks. This brings the total to eight.

One final example before we move on:

K Q J

A 8 5

How many top tricks this time? You have the ace, king, queen and jack
but the answer is *three*, not four. Can you see why? You can only cash
three tricks in the suit, not four, because you have only three cards in
each hand in the suit. Compare that with the club suit in the full hand
given above. There the dummy had four clubs and so, by cashing the
honours in the correct order, *starting with the honour(s) in the hand
with the smaller number of cards in the suit* (South in the hand above),
you could take four tricks. This is another important point to bear in
mind when counting how many tricks you can take.

The next factor to consider is the setting up of tricks. This is the way
to make the extra tricks you need if your top tricks are not sufficient,
which they normally will not be. This is a simple example:

K Q J

8 7 5

How many tricks can you make from this holding, even though there
are no top tricks? Obviously the answer is two. You lead the king, they
take the trick with their ace, and then the queen and jack have become
top tricks. They can be cashed when you regain the lead. So here you
can produce two tricks (the queen and jack), losing one (the king to
the ace) in the process.

What about this suit?

K J 8

Q 7 5

I hope you can see that this is identical to the previous example: there
is one loser and two tricks that can be set up. The fact that the honour
cards are in different hands makes no difference.

Next example:

Q 10 8 7

K J 5

This time there is still only one loser (the ace), but you will set up
three tricks when it has been used to take the king: the queen, jack and
ten will all become winners.

What about this suit?

Q 10 8 7

J 9 4 3

Now the opposition has two top tricks: the ace and the king. But if you lead the queen, which we will assume is taken by the king, and then the jack, which will be captured by the ace, the ten and nine will have become the top cards in the suit. So this suit can produce two tricks, and it has two losers.

When you lead out cards like this in order to set up winners, you are making *suit-establishment* plays.

Suit Combinations

What do you think about this situation?

A Q

3 2

How many tricks will you take from this holding?

— WINNING FINESSE —

Obviously if North has the lead the best you can do is play the ace and hope that the king drops. Not much chance of that if they have nine cards in the suit. (There are thirteen cards in each suit, remember.) But what if South has the lead; what would you do?

You can lead a low card and put up the ace; this will win if either opponent has the singleton king. Not good odds. But what if you lead a low card and, if West plays small, put in the queen? If West hold the king, the queen will win the trick and then you can cash the ace: two tricks in the suit. Of course, if East has the king he will win the queen with it and you will only have one trick. But half the time West will have the king, so half the time you will get two tricks in the suit. This type of play, putting in a lower card in the hope that an honour is well-placed, is called a *finesse*. And the ace-queen, when sitting over the king, is called a *tenace*. The king is trapped in a pincer – the word tenace comes from the Spanish word *tenaza*, which means pincers.

— LOSING FINESSE —

Here is another finessing position:

K J 8

A 3 2

You could try to make three tricks by cashing the ace and king, but
that is against the odds. It is a much better play to take the ace and
then lead the two; if West plays low, put in the jack. If West has the
queen, which he should half the time, you will take three tricks. If East
has the queen, bad luck. But notice that playing out the ace and king is
only a more successful play if East has queen-doubleton, which is
very unlikely. (The king-jack is another tenace, clasping the queen in
its pincers.)

There are variations on these themes:

A 6 5

Q J 10

Run the queen through West and hope that he has the king.

A J 10

K 7 6

This time you can play East or West for the queen, either by cashing
the ace and running the jack, or by cashing the king and playing low to
the jack. This is called a *two-way finesse* because you can finesse
through either opponent.

Now we come to more complicated positions.

A Q 10

4 3 2

How do you play these cards assuming you have lots of entries to the
South hand if you wish to make either two or three tricks?

If you need two tricks, play a low card and put in either the ten or
the queen. (If you cannot afford to lose the lead you must play the
queen, but if you can afford to lose the lead either play will suffice.) If
the ten loses to the king you have your two tricks. But if either the
ten loses to the jack or the queen loses to the king, the second time you
play the suit, put in the other honour. You must make two tricks if
West has either the king or the jack. This is in fact a 76% proposition.

If you need three tricks you must hope that West has both the king
and jack — a 24% chance. Then you lead low to the ten on the first
round, and when that holds, you return to the South hand and play a

low card to the queen. If the sun is shining you will get three tricks, but most of the time it will be like normal British weather: raining; East will have one of the honours. This type of play is called a *double finesse* because you finesse twice.

K J

3 2

If you need one trick you must guess which honour West holds. If he has the queen you must play low to the jack; but if he has the ace you must lead low and put up the king. It is a straight guess, unless, of course, West has both the ace and queen, when you cannot lose.

K J 10

5 3 2

If you need two tricks, hope that West has the queen. Lead low to the ten and after East has won with the ace, get back to the South hand and finesse the jack.

Next example:

A J 10

6 4 2

Play low to the ten, and if that loses to an honour, finesse the jack on the next round. You will make two tricks if West has either the king or queen.

K 10 9

5 3 2

To play for two tricks it is correct to lead low to the nine. If it loses to the jack or queen, play low to the ten the second time.

A Q 9

6 5 4

This one is more difficult. It is correct to play low to the *nine* if you need two tricks. If it loses to the ten or jack, finesse the queen on the second round. But it is possible that this is the position:

A Q 9

J 10 7 2   K 8 3

6 5 4

If you finesse the queen on the first round you will only make one trick; and it cannot cost to put in the nine on the first round unless you need two tricks without surrendering the lead.

                          K J 9

                          5 4 2

If you need two tricks you must guess whether West has the ace and
ten, in which case you must play low to the nine on the first round; or
the ace and queen, in which case you must put in the jack on the first
round; or if he has the queen and ten, in which case you must play the
nine on the first round. Do you now see that in fact it is not a guess
after all? You need to find West with two honours, and the play of the
nine wins in two situations, whereas the play of the jack only works
in one. These are the three positions.

                          K J 9
      A Q 8   10 7 6 3
                          5 4 2

                          K J 9
      A 10 8   Q 7 6 3
                          5 4 2

                          K J 9
      Q 10 8   A 7 6 3
                          5 4 2

Now for some single-suit combinations that are slightly different.

                          K Q J 4

                          8 6 3

How many tricks can you make from this suit, and how do you play it
to try to get the maximum number of tricks?

   The answer is that you should lead towards the honours every time.
If West has the ace you must make three tricks. If East has the ace,
however, you will only take two tricks unless the suit breaks three-three.
It might seem that you could get these tricks by leading the king from
the dummy, but if the cards are like this:

                          K Q J 4
      A 7   10 9 5 2
                          8 6 3

you can hopefully see that it is not the same at all. If you lead the king
from the dummy, West will win with the ace and later East will use the
ten to beat the four. But if you lead the three, which card does West

play? If he puts up the ace, you play dummy's four and the king-queen-jack are all winners. So let us assume that West plays the seven. Not knowing that he has only the ace left, you come back to your hand in a different suit and lead the six. Now West has to play the ace, you follow with the four from the dummy and again collect three tricks.

The moral is: *lead towards honour combinations*.

Here is another:

K Q 8

5 4 2

If you want two tricks, hope West has the ace. Lead low and put up the king, return to hand and lead low again. If West does not play the ace, put up the queen and hope the lay-out is like this:

K Q 8

A 10 7 3   J 9 6

5 4 2

The same thing happens if a suit looks like this:

Q J 5

6 4 2

Wanting one trick in the suit you must hope that West has either the ace or the king (or both). Lead low and play the jack. East wins, say, with the king. When you are back in your hand, play low to the queen and hope West has the ace. This could be the position:

Q J 5

A 9 7 3   K 10 8

6 4 2

Note that if you start by leading the queen from the dummy, West can win with the ace and then East will sit with the king-ten over dummy's jack-five and you will make no tricks.

How do you play this suit to try to win two tricks?

Q 5 3

A 8 7

The correct play is to cash the ace and then lead low to the queen. If you are lucky West will have the king and you will make your two tricks. Why did you not lead the queen from the dummy? Because East will cover if he has the king, and you will only make the ace. (Admittedly you could not make two tricks in this case anyway, but what happens when West has the king? You run the queen, he takes it with the king and again you have one trick only.)

                              A 6 5

                              Q J 7 4
What is the correct play for three tricks?

If you got this one right, well done. You should cash the ace first and then lead low towards the queen-jack. If East plays low on the second round, put up the jack. If it loses, hope the suit breaks three-three, but if it wins, go back to the dummy and play the six. If East plays low again, put up the queen. If West wins the trick the suit must have broken three-three. The finesse can never gain. The lay-out you are hoping for, which will teach the finessers a lesson, is:

                              A 6 5
     10 3   K 9 8 2
                              Q J 7 4
Only by cashing the ace and leading twice towards the queen-jack will you collect three tricks.

Now a couple that are a little more complicated.

                              Q 5 4

                              K 10 7
What is the best play for two tricks?

The answer is to lead towards the queen. If West goes in with the ace, you can score both the queen and king. If, however, the queen loses to the ace, then you must get back to the dummy and lead the four, preparing to finesse the ten.

If the queen wins the trick, lead a small card from the dummy and again finesse the ten. You know when the queen wins that East does not have the ace, so your only hope for two tricks is to finesse the ten, playing East for the jack.

To conclude, you make two tricks if East has either the ace-jack or the jack.

                              J 7 6

                              A K 4 3
What is the best play for three tricks?

The answer is to cash the ace in case either player has a singleton queen, and then to lead low towards the jack. If West has the queen you have your three tricks. But if East takes the jack with the queen you must hope that the suit is three-three. It is wrong to cash the ace and king because that only gains against cashing the ace and leading low towards the jack when East has specifically the doubleton-queen, which is very unlikely.

J 7 6

A K 10 4

Now you can take a finesse, but be careful. Suppose the full distribution is:

J 7 6

9 8 5 2   Q 3

A K 10 4

If you lead the jack from the dummy East will cover with the queen and you will lose a trick to the nine. The correct play is to lead the six and finesse the ten. If that holds, play off the ace. If the queen drops lead low to the jack, but if it does not, cash the king and hope for a three-three break.

(If you find any of these combinations hard to visualise, get out a pack of cards, lay out the North and South hands and try several distributions of the East-West cards to confirm that the recommended play is in fact correct. Or write down all the different possibilities on a piece of paper and confirm that the lines I propose win against the greatest number of possible lay-outs.)

This one is difficult at first.

A J 6 5

Q 4

What is the best play for three tricks?

The answer is to lead low towards the queen. If the queen loses to the king you have had it. But consider when East has the king. If he shoots in with it when you lead low from the dummy you can take three top tricks. But if he plays low and your queen wins, then you should *duck* on the way back, playing for this lay-out:

A J 6 5

10 8 3 2   K 9 7

Q 4

You duck on the second round and lead out the ace on the third, hoping that the king will drop under the ace.

Now there are two positions that will occur countless times if you play this game regularly for years to come.

      (i) A 6 4 2   (ii) A 6 4 2

        K J 5 3   K J 7 5 3

What is the correct play for four tricks in the first situation and five in the second?

In the first you should cash the ace and then finesse the jack on the second round if East does not play the queen. However, with the second the best play is to take the ace and then play low to the king the second time if East plays low again. This has led to a rhyme: 'eight ever, nine never' referring to the finesse. But as with all rules in bridge, treat it with care. Bridge is a game when one can never say 'always'.

Trick Production

The above has told you how to play some suit combinations to best advantage. But normally in no-trump contracts one is wondering how to develop extra tricks. These usually come from the long suits that you have in the hand, and here it helps to be able to count to thirteen. The biggest difference of all between an expert and an average player who could be better is the amount of effort they put in at the table. The expert is thinking the whole time, and is counting furiously. Of course, not all suits need to be counted on every hand, but it is a good habit to get into. The good players are also counting points. For example, if your right-hand opponent opened a weak no-trump, has already shown up with thirteen points and you are faced with a two-way finesse for a queen, what would you do? The poor player would say that it is a guess, but in fact it is a certainty. If your right-hand opponent had that queen it would give him fifteen points, too much for a weak no-trump, so his partner must have the key card. It is this type of logical thought, supported by counting, that makes an expert an expert. When you start playing you will find you have so much to think about; I often compare it with starting to drive a car. But after a short while some things will come naturally and you can give more time and effort to counting during a hand, and your play will improve considerably.

Having had a brief journey down a side road, let us get back to the main highway. Suppose you have a suit of ace-king-to-five opposite three small. How many tricks will it make?

We are considering

AK754

632

If the suit breaks three-two, which it will do most of the time, there are four tricks for the taking. Either play off three rounds if you have the entries, or duck on the first round to maintain communications, and then play out the ace and king. If they were three-two you will be left with numbers twelve and thirteen and can cash them with impunity.

A similar situation that occurs regularly is this one:

K8764

Q32

To try for four tricks, unless you feel sure that West has the ace, lead low from the dummy and put up the queen. When it holds (if it does not you will not make four tricks in the suit), duck on the way back hoping that East began with the doubleton ace. (Obviously you can play the other hand for the doubleton ace but you will be left with the suit blocked by the queen in your hand.) This is the distribution you are hoping for:

K8764
J 10 5   A 9
Q32

QUIZ

1. How many top tricks are there in these suits?

a. AQ10876   b. KQJ10   c. AQJ   d. AQJ

KJ9   9876   K65   K654

2. How many tricks will you make from these suits, and how many losers will you have in the process?

a. AKJ8   b. KJ9   c. J965   d. Q76

Q106   Q7   1087   K54

3. What is the best way to play these suit combinations for three
tricks in each case?

a. K 10 9 6   b. A Q 10   c. A Q 9 6   d. K Q 9 6

   Q 8 5 3   J 6 4   5 3 2   10 8 7

4. In each of these suit combinations, what is the maximum number of
tricks you can make if the cards lie favourably, and what is the minimum number you will end with if the cards lie unfavourably?

a. A Q 10   b. K J 10   c. K Q 9 6 5   d. K J 10 8 7

   6 4 2   7 5 4 3   A 2   9 6 5 4 3 2

Answers on page 190

18   *Play Techniques*

He played the King as though under momentary
apprehension that someone else was about to play the
ace.

Eugene Field

Having looked at the most common suit combinations, we will move on
to the real world of all 52 cards and see how they are manoeuvred.

When playing in a no-trump contract, as soon as the dummy appears,
stop and think. (I know I started the last chapter with this piece of
advice, but it needs emphasising as often as possible because so many
players ignore it.) *Then you should count how many top tricks you
have*. Of course if that gives you what you need for your contract,
fine. Unless they are going to run enough tricks to beat you before you
get the lead, you must make your contract. However, most of the
time you will not find the total equals the number contracted for in
the auction. Then you must try to decide where the extra tricks can
be found. But at the same time you must check that the opposition is
not going to cash enough tricks in their suit(s) to defeat you before
you have had a chance to make your contract.

My first example hand features a suit-establishment play. If you watched the *Join Us For Bridge* programmes, you might recognise this deal.

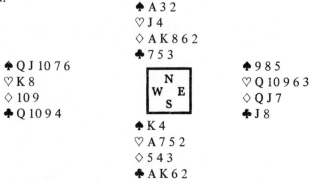

```
                    ♠ A 3 2
                    ♡ J 4
                    ◇ A K 8 6 2
                    ♣ 7 5 3
  ♠ Q J 10 7 6       ┌─────────┐       ♠ 9 8 5
  ♡ K 8              │   N     │       ♡ Q 10 9 6 3
  ◇ 10 9             │ W     E │       ◇ Q J 7
  ♣ Q 10 9 4         │   S     │       ♣ J 8
                    └─────────┘
                    ♠ K 4
                    ♡ A 7 5 2
                    ◇ 5 4 3
                    ♣ A K 6 2
```

Sitting South you arrive in three no-trumps and West leads the queen of spades. How many top tricks do you have? Where will the extra tricks come from?

You have seven top tricks: four aces and three kings. The other two

— HOLD - UP —

tricks can come from the diamond suit if it breaks three-two.

Where will you win the first trick? If you win it in hand you can then play off three rounds of diamonds, setting up the eight and the six as the last two cards in the suit. But if you win the opening trick with the ace of spades you will leave yourself with no entry to the dummy, so you would have to duck the first round of the suit, leading the two from the dummy and playing the three from your hand. (In fact ducking at trick one is the better play wherever you win the opening trick because it makes your communications easier.)

Hold-Up

One of the most important plays in bridge is ducking even though you could have won a trick. In the above hand it is best to duck the first round in the diamond suit. Another aspect of this type of play comes when you hold up a winner in order to annul the power of the opposition's suit.

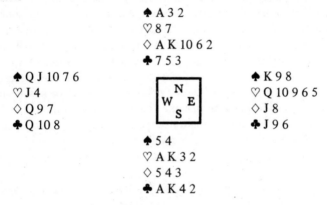

```
                    ♠ A 3 2
                    ♡ 8 7
                    ◇ A K 10 6 2
                    ♣ 7 5 3
  ♠ Q J 10 7 6                        ♠ K 9 8
  ♡ J 4              ┌─────────┐      ♡ Q 10 9 6 5
  ◇ Q 9 7           │    N    │       ◇ J 8
  ♣ Q 10 8         │ W     E │        ♣ J 9 6
                    │    S    │
                    └─────────┘
                    ♠ 5 4
                    ♡ A K 3 2
                    ◇ 5 4 3
                    ♣ A K 4 2
```

Again South is in three no-trumps, again there are seven top tricks and again the queen of spades is led. But do you see the difference? If you take the first trick with the ace and duck a diamond (or play off the ace, the king and another round), the opposition will win the diamond trick and take four spade tricks to defeat your contract by one before you were able to cash your nine tricks. What is the counter to this defence?

The answer is that you should duck the ace of spades until the third round. The position will then be:

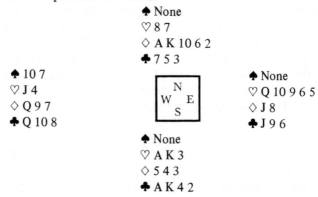

♠ None
♡ 8 7
◇ A K 10 6 2
♣ 7 5 3

♠ 10 7
♡ J 4
◇ Q 9 7
♣ Q 10 8

♠ None
♡ Q 10 9 6 5
◇ J 8
♣ J 9 6

♠ None
♡ A K 3
◇ 5 4 3
♣ A K 4 2

Now if you play off three rounds of diamonds not only will you have no entry to the last two, but also you will have let West gain the lead to cash his two spade winners. The correct play is to cross to the ace of clubs (or hearts) and lead a diamond, finessing the ten if West plays low. (If West plays the queen or jack, win with the king, return to hand in the other suit, hearts, and play another diamond, putting in the ten if West plays low.) East is welcome to that trick but he has no spade to play and you will be able to make nine tricks in comfort.

What if East did have another spade to play? Then the spades will have broken four-four and you will make your contract. (It is normal to lead from your longest suit against a no-trump contract.)

It can also be correct to duck when you have two winners in the suit.

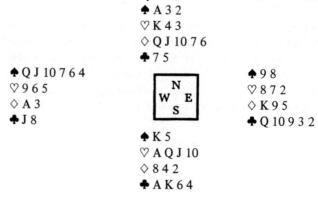

♠ A 3 2
♡ K 4 3
◇ Q J 10 7 6
♣ 7 5

♠ Q J 10 7 6 4
♡ 9 6 5
◇ A 3
♣ J 8

♠ 9 8
♡ 8 7 2
◇ K 9 5
♣ Q 10 9 3 2

♠ K 5
♡ A Q J 10
◇ 8 4 2
♣ A K 6 4

Once more South has to play in three no-trumps and West leads the queen of spades. How many top tricks do you have, and where will the extra(s) come from? Think it over carefully before reading on.

The declarer has eight top tricks: two in spades, four in hearts and two in clubs. The extra trick must come from the diamond suit. But watch what happens if you win the first trick with the king of spades and lead a diamond. If the defenders play well, East will win the first diamond with the king and play his second spade. West will overtake with the ten and what can you do? Whether you duck or go up with the ace, West will win the second round of diamonds with the ace and cash his spade winners to defeat the contract.

But what happens if you duck the first trick? West will persevere with spades, you will win with the king and play a diamond. East can win this with the king but he does not have a spade to play. So when West gets the lead with the ace of diamonds his suit will not be established: the ace is still in the dummy. So you will make three no-trumps instead of going down.

The more you play bridge, the more you will see the dramatic effect a ducking play can have. Keep it in mind while you play.

Keeping Communications

It is important to make sure that you can cash any winners you have set up. This is a simple example.

A K 6 5 4

Q 3

Given that the suit breaks three-three and that North has no entry in a side-suit, how many tricks can you take?

— KEEP COMMUNICATIONS —

Of course the answer is five but only if you *cash the honour in the short hand first*. If you play the queen and then cross to the king, you will be in the North hand to lead the suit from the top down. But if you cash the ace first and then take the queen, you will be in the South hand and the three winners will stay stranded in the dummy unavailable to you.

This hand gives another example of keeping an avenue open to your tricks.

```
        ♠ 7 6 5
        ♡ 6 4
        ◊ A K Q 8 7 6
        ♣ 5 3


        ♠ A K 4
        ♡ A K 5 3
        ◊ 5 2
        ♣ A K Q 4
```

This time the contract is six no-trumps and West leads the queen of hearts (no, not the queen of spades this time!). How many top tricks do you have, and how do you propose to make your contract?

There are ten top tricks and the diamond suit can easily supply the other two. As the five cards the opposition hold will normally break three-two, it looks so simple: win the lead and play off the top diamonds. If they break three-two it will give you all thirteen tricks, not the twelve you contracted for. Suppose the full distribution is like this:

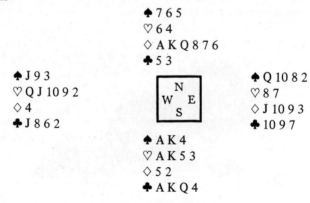

Now when you play off the top diamonds East will be able to win the fourth round and the other two winners you need for your contract will be stranded in the dummy. The solution is to duck the first round of diamonds. Then you can win whatever East returns and run the diamond suit, making the twelve tricks you said you would collect. Is it worth the risk of going down in a slam and not getting the juicy bonuses just for the 30 points one would get for the overtrick if the diamonds were three-two? Of course not.

This hand looks similar to an earlier one, but there is a critical difference.

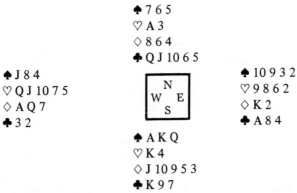

```
                    ♠ 7 6 5
                    ♡ A 3
                    ◊ 8 6 4
                    ♣ Q J 10 6 5
  ♠ J 8 4                              ♠ 10 9 3 2
  ♡ Q J 10 7 5          N              ♡ 9 8 6 2
  ◊ A Q 7          W         E         ◊ K 2
  ♣ 3 2                 S              ♣ A 8 4
                    ♠ A K Q
                    ♡ K 4
                    ◊ J 10 9 5 3
                    ♣ K 9 7
```

Once more three no-trumps, the lead being the queen of hearts. You have five top tricks in the majors and can produce four more in clubs. How should you play? Can you see any snags?

The problem is that the defenders might be able to hold up the ace of clubs until the third round, in which case you will need a dummy entry to the twelfth and thirteenth cards. You cannot duck the opening lead as you have only two cards in each hand, so you must be careful to win with the king in your hand, keeping the ace as the entry to the dummy to allow you to cash the last two club tricks.

Two Chances Are Better Than One
When considering how to produce the extra tricks that you need, look carefully to see if there is more than one way you might get them.

Take this hand for example.

♠ 7 6 5
♡ Q 5 3
◇ A J 7 6 4
♣ 6 5

♠ A
♡ A K 8 4
◇ K 8 5
♣ A K 7 4 2

Your favourite contract: three no-trumps, and a spade lead. How do you try to collect nine tricks?

First of all count the top tricks: eight. So you only need one more trick. This can come either from the hearts breaking three-three or from the diamond finesse working, but you cannot afford to lose the lead because the opposition will surely be able to cash at least four spade tricks.

The correct play is to combine the chances. First of all cross to the queen of hearts, then return to the ace of hearts and cash the king. If the suit breaks three-three take your ninth trick with the eight of hearts and enjoy the luxury of trying to drop the queen of diamonds in two rounds for overtricks. However, if the hearts are not three-three, play off the king of diamonds, lead another diamond and put in the jack from the dummy if West plays low for a second time, offering a silent prayer to your favourite god or goddess. This is the best percentage play in the diamond suit. Of course, if it works and West started with two or three diamonds to the queen you will be able to cash all five diamonds and make eleven tricks.

One more deal that is slightly tougher.

♠ 8 6 4
♡ Q 10 7
◇ A J 7 6 3
♣ 8 5

♠ A
♡ A J 9 8
◇ K 5 4
♣ A K 4 3 2

You guessed it: three no-trumps on a spade lead from West.

This time you have only six top tricks and can make the extra ones that you need if either the heart finesse works or the diamond suit comes home. How should you play?

The secret on a hand like this is to cash the winners in the longer suit, and if the key honour does not drop, finesse in the shorter suit. Here you have seven hearts in both hands, and eight diamonds. So cash the king of diamonds and cross to the ace. If the queen appears you can cash the rest of the diamonds in descending order. But if someone still has that queen, then you take the heart finesse, hoping that it will work. This is the best way of combining the chances on the hand.

Keep The Danger Hand Off The Lead
Occasionally you will have to be careful who gets the lead.

Q 4

K 5 3

Suppose West leads this suit against a no-trump contract. The correct play is to rise with the queen, not to play low from the dummy. If East has the ace he should not play the ace if you put in the four from the dummy. But let us worry about the times that West has the ace. The queen will win the trick, and you will have to play on. What happens if East gets the lead? He will return this suit and West will sit waiting to tread on your king with his ace. But if West has the lead he cannot ruin you in this suit: if he cashes the ace, you play low; if he

— KEEP THE DANGER HAND OFF THE LEAD —

leads a low card you must score the king.

Let us put that suit into a full deal and see how it affects the play.

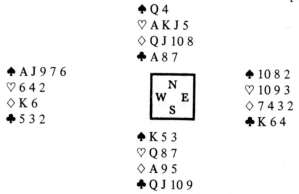

```
                    ♠ Q 4
                    ♡ A K J 5
                    ◇ Q J 10 8
                    ♣ A 8 7
♠ A J 9 7 6                              ♠ 10 8 2
♡ 6 4 2         N                        ♡ 10 9 3
◇ K 6         W   E                      ◇ 7 4 3 2
♣ 5 3 2         S                        ♣ K 6 4
                    ♠ K 5 3
                    ♡ Q 8 7
                    ◇ A 9 5
                    ♣ Q J 10 9
```

The opening spade lead is taken by the queen and you find that you have six top tricks to go with the trick already in the bag. You can finesse in either minor, but the right play is to finesse in diamonds, not clubs. Can you see why? You must keep East off the lead, and if you finesse in clubs East might win with the king and return the ten of spades, allowing the defence to take four spade tricks to defeat the contract. Whereas if you finesse in diamonds West cannot hurt you in spades. If he switches to a club, tempting you to finesse, you must not. Put up the ace and cash your nine tricks.

The Bath Coup

This is a play that is particularly useful in no-trump contracts, but like most manoeuvres, does have its uses when there is a trump suit.

```
                    7 5 4
K Q 10 8 6                              9 3
                    A J 2
```

West leads the king of this suit. If you take the trick with the ace and East is able to regain the lead, he will be able to play his second card and you will get only one trick in the suit. But what happens if you duck at trick one? This is the Bath Coup, which was first played in Bath during the days of whist. If West continues the suit he gives you two tricks in the suit and if he switches East will have to gain the lead to play the suit *and* West will have to regain the lead to cash the tricks. Consider a full deal.

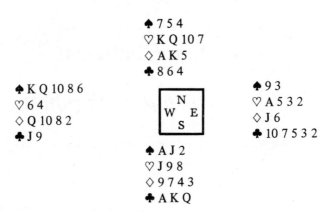

Against three no-trumps West leads the king of spades. If declarer wins with the ace he will go down in the contract. When East wins a trick with the ace of hearts he will return his nine of spades and West will either overtake with the ten, if South plays his two, or will use the queen to capture the jack. But if West is allowed to win the first trick the contract is impregnable.

QUIZ

1. How do you play the following hands in three no-trumps? In each case West leads a low heart.

a.	b.	c.	d.
♠ A K 9	♠ A 5 3	♠ A 6 3	♠ A 4 3
♡ A 7 6	♡ A 6 5	♡ Q 6	♡ 8 7
◇ K J 8	◇ 6 4 3 2	◇ A 10 8 6 4	◇ A 10 8 6 4
♣ Q J 8 7	♣ K 4 3	♣ K 7 6	♣ K 7 6
♠ J 10 7	♠ K Q 2	♠ K 5 4	♠ K 7 5
♡ K J 4	♡ K 7 4	♡ K 5 3	♡ A 6 3
◇ A 7 6	◇ A 7 5	◇ K J 9 7	◇ K J 9 7
♣ 10 9 5 3	♣ A 8 7 5	♣ A 3 2	♣ A 5 4

Answers on page 192

II Suit Contracts

19 *Trump Techniques*

Martin, if dirt were trumps, what hands you would
hold!

Charles Lamb

When you have to play in a suit contract, it is important to realise on
each hand what you should be doing with your trumps. The usual
policy is to draw the oppositions' trumps, which should be at most five
cards in total, and then get on with the side-suits, using your remaining
trumps to ruff any losers in these suits whenever appropriate. This is
a simple hand of that type from *Join Us For Bridge*.

East-West game; dealer South.

♠ Q J 10 6 4
♡ A K 8 3
◇ 4
♣ Q 4 2

♠ 8 7   ♠ 9
♡ J 5 4 2   N   ♡ 10 9
◇ K J 8   W   E ◇ Q 9 7 6 5 3 2
♣ J 10 9 3   S   ♣ A K 6

♠ A K 5 3 2
♡ Q 7 6
◇ A 10
♣ 8 7 5

West	North	East	South
			1♠
No	4♠	No	No
No			

West leads the jack of clubs and there being no point in playing the
queen from the dummy, it holds the first trick. East then takes two
tricks with the king and ace of clubs, before switching to a diamond.

Declarer goes up with the ace, draws trumps in two rounds and cashes the three top hearts, starting with the queen, the honour in the short hand. When the hearts fail to break three-three, he cross-ruffs one heart in hand and one diamond in the dummy, claiming ten tricks.

Naturally that is a straightforward hand. There are some more complicated techniques; I will look at a few of them now.

The Cross-Ruff

This is when you use the trumps in the dummy to ruff losers in your hand, and at the same time use your trumps to ruff dummy's losers.

♠ A Q 10 8 6 4
♡ 9 7 6 5 4 2
◇ A
♣ None

♠ K J 9 7 5 3
♡ None
◇ 2
♣ 9 8 6 4 3 2

The bidding has propelled you into seven spades! They lead a diamond, you win with the ace and see what you can do: the only trump you are missing is the two, so ruff in turn hearts in hand and clubs in the

— CROSS - RUFF —

dummy. That will be thirteen tricks: the ace of diamonds and twelve ruffs. (Do you see which opening lead could have been unfortunate? If West could have led the two of trumps it would have cut down your trumps. If you think your opponents might be about to employ a cross-ruff it is always right to lead a trump. In this case, though, it probably would have made no difference. After four or five ruffs, one of the suits, hearts or clubs, would be set up — the opponents would have no cards left in the suit and the set-up winners need not be ruffed.)

Setting Up a Side-Suit

This is a very common play-technique. In one hand you have a longish suit that is not set up (in other words, it is not all top tricks), but if you ruff one or two cards of the suit in one hand, then the opposition will have no cards left and the small cards remaining will be top tricks. Here is an example.

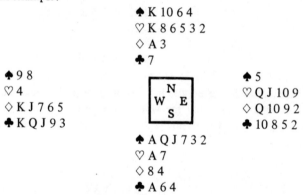

```
                    ♠ K 10 6 4
                    ♡ K 8 6 5 3 2
                    ◇ A 3
                    ♣ 7
  ♠ 9 8                              ♠ 5
  ♡ 4             ┌─────────┐        ♡ Q J 10 9
  ◇ K J 7 6 5    │    N    │        ◇ Q 10 9 2
  ♣ K Q J 9 3    │ W     E │        ♣ 10 8 5 2
                 │    S    │
                 └─────────┘
                    ♠ A Q J 7 3 2
                    ♡ A 7
                    ◇ 8 4
                    ♣ A 6 4
```

Some aggressive bidding gets South into seven spades and West leads the king of clubs. Naturally you can ruff the club losers in the dummy, but what about that diamond loser? The only parking place for that diamond is on the heart suit in the dummy. The correct play is to win the club lead with the ace and draw the trumps. Then play the ace of hearts (the honour from the short hand first, remember), cross to the king of hearts and ruff a heart. Unfortunately that has not set up the suit because East started with four cards in hearts. This is now the position:

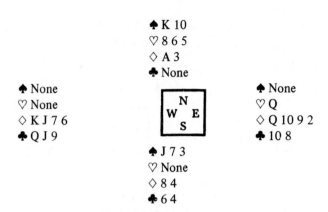

At this point play a diamond to the ace and ruff another heart. Then you return to the dummy by ruffing a club and cash the last two hearts, discarding your small diamond and small club. Finally, you ruff dummy's diamond loser as you no longer have any in your hand and claim.

The Ruffing Finesse

We have looked at the normal finessing positions, but there is one other that is only possible if you have some trumps. This is a classical lay-out:

A Q J 10

6

Instead of leading the six and finessing the ten, you play the six, put up the ace and then lead the queen. If East covers with the king, you ruff and have two winners in the dummy. But if East plays low, you discard and even if West wins with the king, you can throw two more losers a moment later.

Here is a full hand featuring the ruffing finesse.

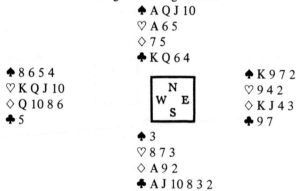

                  ♠ A Q J 10
                  ♡ A 6 5
                  ◇ 7 5
                  ♣ K Q 6 4

♠ 8 6 5 4   ♠ K 9 7 2
♡ K Q J 10   ♡ 9 4 2
◇ Q 10 8 6   ◇ K J 4 3
♣ 5   ♣ 9 7

                  ♠ 3
                  ♡ 8 7 3
                  ◇ A 9 2
                  ♣ A J 10 8 3 2

South plays in five clubs and West leads the king of hearts. You are faced with two losing hearts and a diamond loser. After drawing trumps you could take the spade finesse, hoping that it will win and allow you to throw a heart on the ace. But if it loses then the defenders will cash two heart tricks to defeat the contract. The correct play after drawing trumps is to cross to the ace of spades and lead the queen. If East plays low, throw a heart loser. If West wins with the king he can cash one heart trick, but you will be able to throw the two diamond losers on the two spade winners in the dummy. In fact East will cover the queen of spades with the king, so you ruff, return to dummy with a trump and throw the two heart losers on the jack and ten of spades, conceding just one diamond trick. A slam on 25 high-card points; whatever next?

The techniques that we considered in the section on no-trumps: finessing, hold-up, keeping the wrong opponent off the lead and so on, all apply at times in suit contracts. But there is one factor to consider when approaching the play of the hand at trick one when you have a trump suit: count not only your top tricks but also *count your losers*. When I am playing in a no-trump contract I always note my top tricks first and then see where the other tricks can come from before checking that they will not be taking enough winners to defeat me. But when considering a suit contract I always count the losers first. This gives me a good idea of what I should be doing with my trumps. If the losers total does not exceed the number I can afford, I can usually draw trumps and get on with taking my tricks. But if the losers total is too high then I often have to use my trumps to ruff losers, or set up a side-suit to produce discards.

Have a go at these quiz hands, but be careful; the odd one is quite tricky.

QUIZ

1. In these four problems the contract is four spades and West has led a low diamond. How would you play each hand?

a. ♠ K 9 6 4	b. ♠ J 7 6	c. ♠ J 10 9 6 5	d. ♠ Q10975
♡ 7 6 5	♡ 8 6	♡ A Q 4	♡ A 6
◇ A Q	◇ A 6 4	◇ A 6	◇ A 6
♣ A J 8 7	♣ 9 7 6 3 2	♣ 9 6 5	♣ K J 5 3
♠ A Q J 8 7	♠ A K Q 10 9	♠ K Q 8 7 4 3 2	♠ K J 8 6 3 2
♡ K 4 2	♡ A 5 4	♡ K 3	♡ 8 4
◇ 7 5	◇ K J 5	◇ 9 5	◇ 7 5 3 2
♣ K Q 6	♣ 5 4	♣ 4 3	♣ Q

Answers on page 195

III Defensive Methods

20 *Basic Defensive Techniques*

αυδρα μοι εννεπε, Μουσα, πολυτροπον
Tell me, Muse, of the man of many tricks.

Homer

So far we have looked at bidding and card-play, but now we must consider defence. Good defence is perhaps the hardest part of the game because it requires excellent co-operation between the two defenders.

The keys to good defence are:

(a) good visualisation of the declarer's and your partner's hands with particular reference to the distribution of these hands

(b) counting

(c) accurate signalling.

Let us look at these in order. Hand distributions fall into one of two categories: odds or evens, as I call them. You will either have three suits that have an odd number of cards in them and one that has an even number (a void counts as even), or three evens and one odd. Here are the more common hand distributions, confirm for yourself that what I have put is true: 4-4-3-2, 4-3-3-3, 5-3-3-2, 5-4-3-1, 5-4-4-0, 6-4-2-1, 6-4-3-0, 5-5-2-1, 5-5-3-0, and so on.

Whenever you pick up your cards after the deal, count not only the points but also say to yourself your suit distribution. Do that every time and you will find that counting the hands gets easier because not only must your hand have an accepted pattern, but so must each suit round the table. If you have four clubs, dummy three and your partner three, the declarer must have three as well: 4-3-3-3. If you have one diamond, dummy has six and partner holds three, the declarer must have three: 6-3-3-1. If you practise this on every hand you will find that counting, *b* on my list, becomes easier.

During every hand you must try to work out the holdings of both your partner and the declarer. Obviously if you know what they hold from the information you have received both from the signals given to you by your partner and the line of play adopted by the declarer, you will find making the best plays far easier than if you have no idea what anyone holds and you are in effect guessing.

Let us see how you and your partner can signal information across the table in a legal fashion. It starts with the opening lead.

Opening Leads

The choice of the correct opening lead at trick one can often make the difference between beating a contract and letting it make. So it helps to have some idea of what to do.

Not only is the opening lead aimed at aiding the defence, it should also pass information to partner. The declarer, once the dummy comes down, can see all 26 cards at his disposal whereas each defender can only see his cards and half the oppositions'. Naturally this gives the declarer a big advantage, and to try to equalise the score, the defenders are allowed to make the opening lead. So it is a good idea to try to be as effective as possible with your opening lead.

First of all I will describe the different opening leads, leaving a discourse on how one decides what to lead until afterwards.

When you have at least two honours in a combination, at least two of which are touching, it is accepted that you lead the top of the touching honours. Here is a table of some of the different possibilities.

Combination	Lead
A K	Ace
K Q	King
Q J	Queen
J 10	Jack
A Q J	Queen
A J 10	Jack
K J 10	Jack
K 10 9	Ten
Q 10 9	Ten

Two points: you can have more cards in the suit; so from A K 8 7 lead the ace, and so on. If you lead an honour it denies the honour directly above it, but, unless you have led an ace or king, you could still have a higher honour. For example, the lead of the jack denies the queen, but you could have the king or ace.

When you do not have an honour combination, or decide not to lead from one, then you lead a spot card. The normal rules are:

   (i)   higher card from a doubleton
  (ii)   middle card from three small; bottom from three to an honour
 (iii)   fourth highest from four or more cards.
Here are some of the possibilities:

Holding	Lead
8 7	Eight
8 7 5	Seven
Q 5 4	Four
10 8 7 4	Four
K J 6 3	Three
K J 8 7 4	Seven

Note that in these cases you have been given all the cards held in a suit.

When holding a doubleton you lead the top card and then play the second, lower one. With three small cards you lead the middle one, then you play the top one, and finally you contribute the bottom card. This convention is called *MUD*, standing for Middle, Up, Down.

When holding four or more cards, lead the fourth highest, and then follow upwards if you started with four cards, but play a lower one (the fifth or sixth card) if you had a longer suit (five or six cards in it).

The advantage of leading fourth best from four or more cards is that it allows the partner of the opening leader to glean some information about the suit when the dummy appears. Assume your partner has led the four, and this is what you can see:

$$\heartsuit \text{ J 7 6 5 (dummy)}$$

$$\heartsuit \text{ K 10 8 (you)}$$

Assuming the four is fourth best, how many cards does the declarer have in the suit? You know that partner has four, five or six cards (the three and two are missing). This tells you that the declarer has either two, one or no cards in the suit. Next question: what about the number of cards the declarer has that are bigger than the four? If your partner's four is fourth best, he has three cards above the four. There are ten cards in a suit bigger than a four, and you can see seven of them: the dummy has four and you have three. So the declarer has *no* cards bigger than the four! Your partner holds the A Q 9 4 in the suit, and perhaps the two or the three or both of them. So if the declarer plays the five from the dummy, you can confidently play the eight if you are sure partner has led fourth best.

Do you have to do this sort of calculation every time? Yes and no. You do, but there is something to help you called the *Rule of Eleven*: if your partner has led his fourth highest, subtract the value of the card from eleven and that tells you how many cards there are above the card led in the other three hands.

Here are a couple of examples. In each case calculate how many cards the declarer has above the one led, assuming that that card is fourth highest.

a.   ♠ 8 6 4

    ♠ 5 led   ♠ K J 3

b.   ◇ Q 9 6

    ◇ 2 led   ◇ K 8 5 4

As the five has been led in *a*, there are six cards in the other three hands above the five (11-5 = 6). There are four between the dummy and East, so the declarer has two.

In *b* the answer is also two because there are nine cards bigger than the two, and there are seven of them visible in the dummy and East's hand.

Choice of Opening Lead

Obviously it is not easy to give you advice so that you will always find the killing opening lead; every hand is different. But there are some general guidelines which work most of the time.

Against a no-trump contract, lead from your longest suit. If you have an honour combination with at least two honours in it (AKQ or KJ10 etc.), lead the correct honour, the one given in the table earlier in this chapter. Otherwise lead your fourth highest.

Quick quiz: given that you are about to lead from these holdings, which should you choose?

a. K Q 10 7 6   b. K J 10 6   c. K J 7 5   d. K 10 6 4 2

Answers: *a* the king: an honour combination; *b* the jack: another honour combination; *c* the five: fourth best, the two honours do not make an honour combination as they are not touching; *d* the four: fourth best.

These leads tend to be avoided if the opposition has shown length in the suit you are contemplating leading. In that case try the longest suit you hold that they have not bid.

If your partner has bid a suit, lead it unless you really do have a good reason not to. If he has overcalled in a suit, lead it unless you can see the setting tricks yourself. He should not overcall without a good suit, and it is good for partnership morale (about which you will soon learn when you start playing!) if you lead his suit.

Against a suit contract there are more things to consider.

If you have an honour combination in an unbid suit, it is normally right to lead it, but *never underlead an ace*, that is, leading a lower card from a suit headed by the ace; e.g. the jack from A J 10 3. If you think you should lead that suit, lead the ace. Why? Just consider what happens if the declarer has the singleton king in his hand or the dummy; you will never make your ace if you underlead it.

If leading from a long suit, lead fourth highest as before, but *never underlead an ace*.

It is often correct to lead a singleton or a doubleton in an effort to get a ruff.

It is rarely right to lead from three small.

Always consider leading a trump, but do not always lead a trump!

How do you decide which lead to make? First of all, in general lead your partner's suit if he has bid one, particularly as an overcall. Second, decide whether the opponents sound as though they have points to spare for their bidding. If it seems as though they have extras, make an attacking lead. But if they were stretching to reach the contract, try to make a passive lead.

What is the difference between the two? An attacking lead is when you underlead honours, there being a risk that you will give them a free trick. Suppose you lead low from four to the king-jack. If they have the queen and the ace they will be able to make two tricks, and you might never make your king, which you would have done if you had not led the suit. But, of course, if partner has the ace or the queen, your lead will be effective, either cashing tricks if he has the ace, or setting up tricks if he has the queen.

Leading a singleton or doubleton hoping to get a ruff is also an attacking lead, as is leading from an honour combination. In every case you are trying to generate tricks for your side while taking the risk that you will be giving away a trick or two. To use a chess term: you are playing a gambit.

A passive lead is one that is unlikely to give away a trick, but at the same time will not normally produce one. In this category go trump leads, and leads from long suits not headed by an honour or honours.

As I have already said, to judge which is correct, listen to the bidding and try to decide if they have points to spare. If it seems that they do (someone was contemplating making a slam-try over a game bid), make an attacking lead. However, if they struggled along (1♠-2♠-3♠-No), make a passive lead and let them get on with it.

Opening leads are something which improve with experience, but even top players do not get them right all the time.

Returning Partner's Lead
After partner has led a suit, if you get in and decide to lead back that suit, there are methods that you should use to tell partner how many cards you have in that suit. If you started with three cards in the suit, so that you now have two left, you should return the higher one. But if you started with four, you should return the bottom one of the three you have left. This will tell partner how many cards you have, he can see his own hand and the dummy's, so he can work out how many the declarer had.

For example:

$$\diamond\ 6\ 4\ 2\ \text{(dummy)}$$

$$\diamond\ J\ 7\ 5\ \text{(you)}$$

Partner leads the three, say, dummy plays the two and you put up the jack, declarer winning, let us assume, with the queen. In a moment you gain the lead and decide to return this suit: play the seven.

$$\diamond\ 6\ 4\ 2$$

$$\diamond\ J\ 9\ 7\ 5$$

Again partner leads the three, dummy plays the two, you contribute the jack and declarer wins with the queen. When you get in, play back the five, your original fourth best.

Signalling to Partner
Above we have seen how one can tell partner about the number of cards held in a suit, either by leading fourth best, or playing high then low with a doubleton, or following MUD, or by the card returned in a suit partner has led. This did not cover the subject completely, as no doubt you will have guessed. Let us assume that the declarer is in

four spades and that this is the heart suit on two different deals.

a.   ♡ Q 8 7
           ♡ A K 10 5   ♡ 9 4
                                       ♡ J 6 3 2

b.   ♡ Q 8 7
           ♡ A K 10 5   ♡ 9 4 2
                                       ♡ J 6 3

In *a* partner leads the ace (from ace-king) and can give us a ruff on the third round; whereas in *b* it might be better for him to switch to save a tempo, leaving the declarer to play the suit again if he wishes to set up a trick for himself. But how will partner know whether we have two cards or three in the suit? Once again we *signal* the information to him. If one plays a high card before a lower one (this is called a *peter* or an *echo*) it shows an *even number* of cards in the suit. Whereas if one plays in ascending order it shows an odd number of cards in the suit. So in *a* you play the nine under the ace, but in *b* you drop the two. Of course partner will not be sure in *a* whether you have two or four cards in the suit, unless from the bidding he knows that South has four hearts, but at least he knows that you might have a doubleton and therefore that he might be able to give you a ruff on the third round.

If the declarer plays a suit it is also possible to peter to show an even number or to play upwards to indicate an odd number, but be careful that first of all your partner is watching (there is no point in signalling to a blind man) and second that your signal will not be of greater benefit to the declarer than to your partner. For this reason it is often safer not to make a *count signal* unless you are sure your partner needs to know, as in this situation:

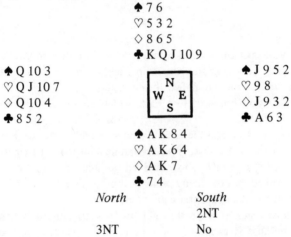

```
                    ♠ 7 6
                    ♡ 5 3 2
                    ◇ 8 6 5
                    ♣ K Q J 10 9
  ♠ Q 10 3                          ♠ J 9 5 2
  ♡ Q J 10 7          N             ♡ 9 8
  ◇ Q 10 4         W     E          ◇ J 9 3 2
  ♣ 8 5 2             S             ♣ A 6 3
                    ♠ A K 8 4
                    ♡ A K 6 4
                    ◇ A K 7
                    ♣ 7 4
```

North	South
	2NT
3NT	No

Your partner, West, leads the queen of hearts; declarer wins with the king and plays a club. How do you defend? Looking at all four hands you can see that you must duck the first club trick (otherwise the declarer can make ten tricks) but take the second trick (otherwise the declarer has eight tricks). If you do exactly that you can hold South to his seven tricks: two spades, two hearts, two diamonds and one club. But what if the full deal is in fact like this?

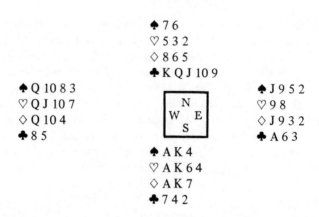

♠ 7 6
♡ 5 3 2
◇ 8 6 5
♣ K Q J 10 9

♠ Q 10 8 3   ♠ J 9 5 2
♡ Q J 10 7   ♡ 9 8
◇ Q 10 4   ◇ J 9 3 2
♣ 8 5   ♣ A 6 3

♠ A K 4
♡ A K 6 4
◇ A K 7
♣ 7 4 2

Now if you take the second round of clubs the declarer will make ten tricks (three ace-kings and four club tricks), whereas if you duck until the third round you will defeat the contract.

How do you know, sitting East, which deal it is? The answer, of course, is that partner tells you. With three clubs in the first hand he plays the two first and then the five, in ascending order to show an odd number of cards. But if it is the second deal he plays the eight first and then the five, a peter to show an even number of clubs. In either case you can calculate how many clubs South has and win a trick with the ace of clubs at the appropriate moment.

In those hands it is clearly right for West to show how many clubs he has because it cannot do any harm: if South has the ace all will become clear as the clubs are run anyway, and if East has it he must be told when it is correct to win a trick with it. However, as I have said, it is usually safer not to signal length unless you are sure partner needs to know. Consider this hand.

North-South game; dealer South.

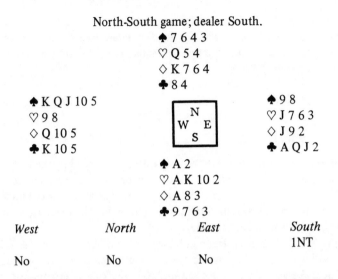

♠ 7 6 4 3
♡ Q 5 4
◇ K 7 6 4
♣ 8 4

♠ K Q J 10 5
♡ 9 8
◇ Q 10 5
♣ K 10 5

♠ 9 8
♡ J 7 6 3
◇ J 9 2
♣ A Q J 2

♠ A 2
♡ A K 10 2
◇ A 8 3
♣ 9 7 6 3

West	North	East	South
			1NT
No	No	No	

West leads the king of spades and South ducks on principle, but he has to win the second round. He has six top tricks and the best chance of a seventh is to make four heart tricks. So at trick three he plays the king of hearts, trying to look like a man without the ace, before crossing to the queen of hearts and playing a third round towards his hand. If East and West are inveterate signallers the declarer will know that both of them have an even number, so when East follows on the third round, the declarer will finesse the ten of hearts and make his contract. But if neither defender is signalling the declarer will have a guess that he will probably get wrong. (It is more likely that the hearts were originally three-three than West having two and East four; and if declarer finesses the ten and it loses to the jack, the defenders will be able to take a lot of tricks in the black suits to defeat the contract by several tricks, whereas if South goes up with the king and the jack does not drop, he can cash out for only one down. That might sound a little complicated, but you will get used to thinking like that the more you play bridge.)

If you are not signalling the count to your partner, how are you transmitting information across the table? There is another type of signal that can be made; I call it the 'likey-no likey' signal. You make an encouraging or discouraging signal to tell your partner that either you like or dislike his lead, or that if he gets in you would like him to play or not to play a particular suit. How do you make an encouraging/

discouraging signal? If you wish to *encourage* in a suit you drop an *unnecessarily high card*, whereas to discourage you drop your lowest card. Here is a simple example. Assume that the contract is three no-trumps in both cases.

a.   ♠ 7 5 4 (dummy)
   ♠ K led   ♠ J 9 2 (you)

b.   ♠ 7 5 4
   ♠ K led   ♠ 9 6 2

You know your partner has the king-queen. In *a*, holding the jack, you would like him to continue the suit, so drop the nine, an unnecessarily high card. Whereas in *b* you are afraid partner is about to fall into the Bath Coup, perhaps with fatal consequences for the defence, so drop the two, the lowest card you have.

In general, if partner leads an honour and you hold the one above or below the sequence he has guaranteed (the queen opposite the lead of the ace; the ace or jack opposite the king; the king or ten opposite the queen) it is correct to encourage (unless, of course, you can see from your hand that it is better for him to switch to a different suit; always consider the hand as a whole, not each suit in isolation). If you do not have a key honour, discourage.

The same signal can be given to try to get partner to switch to a particular suit in the middle of the play.

East-West game; dealer South.

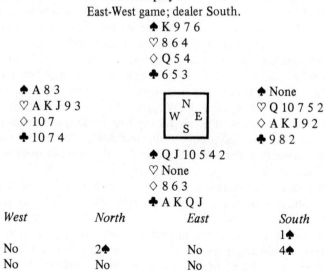

	♠ K 9 7 6		
	♡ 8 6 4		
	◇ Q 5 4		
	♣ 6 5 3		

♠ A 8 3   ♠ None
♡ A K J 9 3   ♡ Q 10 7 5 2
◇ 10 7   ◇ A K J 9 2
♣ 10 7 4   ♣ 9 8 2

♠ Q J 10 5 4 2
♡ None
◇ 8 6 3
♣ A K Q J

West	North	East	South
			1♠
No	2♠	No	4♠
No	No	No	

Both West and East allow the vulnerability to keep them out of the bidding. South has fifteen points counting the length in spades, but when he hears about the spade support from partner he adds three more for his void and has enough to jump to game.

West leads the ace of hearts, dummy plays the four, and East, not knowing that the declarer has a void, drops the ten to show the queen: an unnecessarily high card to encourage in the suit. However, South ruffs and plays the queen of spades. West takes his ace and East has to find a discard; what should he throw? He knows that a diamond switch is imperative, so he drops the *nine* of diamonds, an unnecessarily high card. (In general a six or higher will normally be considered a high card, but you have to watch the cards that are played to see when any given spot card can be taken as high or low.) West switches obediently to the ten of diamonds and three tricks are cashed in the suit to defeat four spades. Note that if West does not switch to diamonds the declarer will be able to draw trumps and throw one of dummy's diamonds on the fourth round of clubs, thus making the contract when he ruffs the third round of diamonds in the dummy.

What would happen if East's diamonds were in fact ◇ A K J 3 2, rather than ◇ A K J 9 2? If he discarded the three of diamonds on the first round of spades it would not look like a high card to West and he would switch to clubs. How can East get around this problem? The answer is to discourage in clubs by dropping the two. Having told your partner that you do not want a club played, he should switch to a diamond. So if there is a choice of two suits, you can either encourage in one of them or discourage in the other for the same result.

To recap: I recommend that you make encouraging/discouraging signals unless you realise that partner needs to know the count in a suit.

The only exception to this rule comes when defending against a suit contract. If your partner leads a high honour in a side-suit, peter with a doubleton. He might think you are indicating the key honour (for example, the ace or jack if he has led the king), but if he plays a third round your ruff will be equivalent. Here is an example:

Game all; dealer South.

```
                    ♠ J 10 8 7
                    ♡ A 9 4
                    ◇ Q 7 4
                    ♣ 9 7 6
    ♠ A 6                              ♠ 5 3
    ♡ K Q 8 5        ┌─────────┐       ♡ 7 2
    ◇ 10 9 6 3       │   N     │       ◇ K J 8 2
    ♣ J 10 5         │ W   E   │       ♣ K Q 8 4 3
                     │   S     │
                     └─────────┘
                    ♠ K Q 9 4 2
                    ♡ J 10 6 3
                    ◇ A 5
                    ♣ A 2
```

West	North	East	South
			1♠
No	2♠	No	3♡
No	3♠	No	No
No			

South makes his natural opening bid and North gives a single raise. Reassessing his count, South comes up with seventeen (one for the fifth spade and one for each doubleton), which means he is just worth a game-try. He bids the suit in which he would like help, but North has an unattractive minimum with the worst possible distribution for a suit contract; he signs off rapidly.

Even though he knows South has some hearts, he also knows that they are not strong ones, so West leads the king of hearts. North wins with the ace while East drops the seven. He does not have the jack, so he would not normally encourage, but as he has a doubleton there is a chance he can get a ruff, so he peters.

At trick two a trump is played from the dummy, South putting up the king and West winning with the ace. Having seen the seven of hearts at trick one, West hopes his partner has either the jack or a doubleton, so he cashes the queen of hearts and plays a third round. East is able to ruff this trick, and together with two tricks in the minors, the contract goes one down. If East had played the two of hearts at trick one, which would be the correct card if the contract were in no-trumps, West might not have continued with hearts when in with the ace of spades, thus allowing three spades to make, the heart ruff being the fifth trick for the defence.

Suit Preference Signal

There is one other signal you can give to your partner, and it occurs when you know you are about to give your partner a ruff. If you have a re-entry, you want to make sure your partner returns the correct suit so that you can give him another ruff. This is done by making a *suit preference signal*, which was originally suggested by an American, Hy Lavinthal, but was popularised by another American, William McKenney, so it is often called a *McKenney* signal.

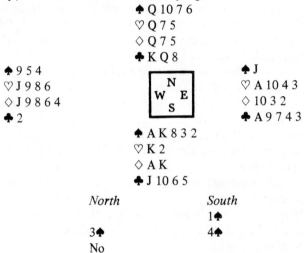

♠ Q 10 7 6
♡ Q 7 5
◇ Q 7 5
♣ K Q 8

♠ 9 5 4
♡ J 9 8 6
◇ J 9 8 6 4
♣ 2

♠ J
♡ A 10 4 3
◇ 10 3 2
♣ A 9 7 4 3

♠ A K 8 3 2
♡ K 2
◇ A K
♣ J 10 6 5

North	South
	1♠
3♠	4♠
No	

West leads his singleton club, East wins with the ace, gives his partner a ruff, gets back in with the ace of hearts and another club ruff defeats the contract. But what if the full deal had been like this?

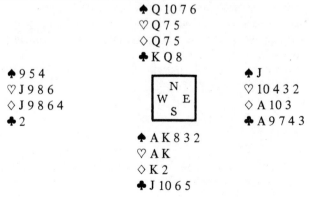

♠ Q 10 7 6
♡ Q 7 5
◇ Q 7 5
♣ K Q 8

♠ 9 5 4
♡ J 9 8 6
◇ J 9 8 6 4
♣ 2

♠ J
♡ 10 4 3 2
◇ A 10 3
♣ A 9 7 4 3

♠ A K 8 3 2
♡ A K
◇ K 2
♣ J 10 6 5

This time West must play a diamond at trick three in order to get his second ruff. How does West tell which hand it is? The answer is that his partner, East, gives him a suit preference signal. For this purpose the suit in which the ruff is being given is ignored, and so is the trump suit. That leaves two suits, hearts and diamonds in the above deals, to worry about. If East, when giving his partner the ruff, wants the higher-ranking suit returned (hearts above), he returns an unnecessarily high club when giving the ruff: the nine in hand one. But if East wants the lower-ranking suit returned (diamonds in our example), he plays his lowest club when giving the ruff: the three in deal two. By noting which club his partner plays, West knows which suit to return in order to get the critical second ruff.

One word of warning about suit preference signals: they come up very infrequently, and you must be sure your partner will read your signal as suit preference and not as encouraging/discouraging or count. Tread the thin ice very carefully.

And one word of advice: watch those spot cards! It is no good partner giving you a suit preference signal if you are not taking note of all the cards that are being played. At times a seven will be his lowest card, or a four his highest. To play bridge well you must remember the critical cards that are played. I do it by saying each one to myself as it is played. So if I were West in the first of the hands given above, I would say, 'Two of clubs, king, ace and five. Nine of clubs, six, four of spades, eight of clubs.

'Partner returned the nine; is that low or high? I have not seen the jack, the ten, the seven, the four and the three. But as declarer has played the five and six, and he opened one spade, not one club, which he would do with five-five in the black suits, I think that nine must be a high card. Therefore, I must return a heart, not a diamond.'

There was a suit preference signal in the penultimate programme of *Join Us For Bridge*, but it was to no avail after careful play by the declarer.

Game all; dealer East.

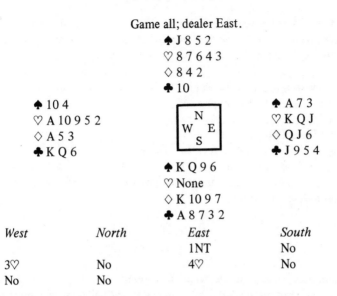

| ♠ J 8 5 2 |
| ♡ 8 7 6 4 3 |
| ◇ 8 4 2 |
| ♣ 10 |

♠ 10 4
♡ A 10 9 5 2
◇ A 5 3
♣ K Q 6

♠ A 7 3
♡ K Q J
◇ Q J 6
♣ J 9 5 4

♠ K Q 9 6
♡ None
◇ K 10 9 7
♣ A 8 7 3 2

West	North	East	South
		1NT	No
3♡	No	4♡	No
No	No		

North decided to lead her singleton club, perhaps inadvisedly with all five trumps. (On a spade lead the contract would be more awkward.) However, South went up with the ace of clubs at trick one, and declarer carefully unblocked the queen. South returned the *eight* of clubs, his highest card asking for a spade back. Declarer played the king of clubs, North ruffed and obediently switched to a spade, but the declarer rose with dummy's ace, drew trumps in four rounds (overtaking dummy's jack with his ace in the process), and played the carefully preserved six of clubs in this position:

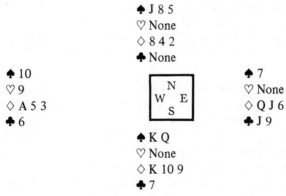

♠ J 8 5
♡ None
◇ 8 4 2
♣ None

♠ 10
♡ 9
◇ A 5 3
♣ 6

♠ 7
♡ None
◇ Q J 6
♣ J 9

♠ K Q
♡ None
◇ K 10 9
♣ 7

The ten of spades was thrown on the nine of clubs, and the diamond finesse taken. Even though that won there was still a diamond loser and so four hearts was made exactly to clinch the rubber.

That covers signalling. To conclude the theory in this chapter, five important defensive techniques.

Second Hand Low
If you are the second player to contribute a card to a trick, your partner will be the last to do so. In this situation it is usually correct to play a low card, leaving it up to your partner to try to win the trick. Here is a simple example.

$$♡ J 7 6$$

$$♡ A 10 9 4 \qquad\qquad ♡ Q 8 5$$

$$♡ K 3 2$$

If the dummy leads the six, what is the point of putting up the queen? If you do that the declarer will cover with the king and make a trick with his jack. But if you contribute the five he will probably play his king, hoping you have the ace, and will take no tricks in the suit.

If you are sitting West and the declarer makes the unusual play of a low one towards the dummy, play small. If you go up with the ace you will set up his king, but if you play low you will ensure that the declarer makes no tricks in the suit.

Like all bridge sayings, 'second hand low' is not without its exceptions. The most common time when it is wrong to play second hand low occurs if you hold an honour sequence and risk giving the declarer a cheap trick if you play low. For example:

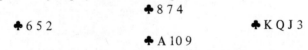

$$♣ 8 7 4$$

$$♣ 6 5 2 \qquad\qquad\qquad ♣ K Q J 3$$

$$♣ A 10 9$$

Declarer calls for the four from the dummy; if you play low he might finesse the nine and win a surprising trick. You must put in an honour to stop that happening.

Which honour should you play? When leading from an honour sequence you should start with the top of touching honours, but *when following suit play the lower/lowest of touching honours*. So in the above example, play the jack. When declarer takes this with the ace, your partner will know that you do not have the ten and that you have the queen, perhaps with the king as well.

Third Hand High

It follows naturally that if the first two players have contributed low cards, the third player normally makes a serious effort to win the trick, to stop the fourth player winning it unnecessarily cheaply.

— SECOND HAND LOW , THIRD HAND HIGH —

♠ 8 6 4

♠ Q 10 7 2   ♠ K 9 3

♠ A J 5

If your partner, West, leads the two in this suit and dummy contributes the four, you must put up the king to stop the declarer making two tricks in the suit. Later you will be able to lead through the declarer's jack to your partner's queen-ten tenace.

♡ 8 6 4

♡ J 9 7 2   ♡ K Q 3

♡ A 10 5

Again partner leads the two and dummy puts on the four; which card
do you play sitting East? As I said above, when following suit you
should play the lower of two touching honours: in this case the queen.
If you play the king it denies holding the queen.

Exceptions? Yes, of course there are exceptions. The most common
one is when dummy has an honour but does not play it at trick one.

♢ Q 6 4

♢ J 9 7 2   ♢ K 10 3

♢ A 8 5

Partner leads the two and declarer plays a small card from the dummy;
you should put in the *ten*. If it is a suit contract you know that partner
cannot have the ace, so if you put up the king the declarer must be able
to make two tricks in the suit. Whereas if you put in the ten, finessing
against the dummy, there is a chance you can hold him to one trick if
lay-out is as given above.

If it is a no-trump contract you must give declarer a trick if you play
the king at trick one. If your partner has led from ♢ A J 7 2 he will not
be pleased.

♣ J 6 4

♣ K 10 7 2   ♣ Q 9 3

♣ A 8 5

Partner, West, leads the two and dummy plays the four; can you see
why you should put in the nine, not the queen? You know that your
partner does not have both the ace and king because he would have led
the ace, not the two. So declarer has one or both of them — certainly
the ace if this is a side-suit and the contract is not in no-trumps, or the
ace or king if the contract is being played in no-trumps. If you put up
the queen the declarer will win with his honour and be able to play
a second round towards dummy's jack to produce a second trick in
the suit. If you play the nine and partner has led from the ace or king
with the ten as well, you can restrict the declarer to one trick in the suit.

Lead Up To Weakness
If you are sitting over the dummy (East in all our examples), have the

lead in the middle of the hand and are not sure what to play, it is usually correct to lead dummy's weakest suit: lead up to weakness. Because the fourth hand to play has no high cards in the suit, it will normally be easier for your side to win a trick.

♣ 6 4 3

♣ A Q 5   ♣ 10 9 8 7

♣ K J 2

Switch to the ten of clubs, the top of a sequence. If the declarer plays an honour, your partner will win the trick. Then if you regain the lead, you can play the nine and the declarer will get no tricks in the suit.

Lead Through Strength

The corollary of the previous section is that, unless your side has all the high cards in a suit, if you are leading up to weakness, you are also leading through strength. This will be more apparent in the example given above if we switch the hands round, making the South hand the dummy:

♣ K J 2

♣ 10 9 8 7   ♣ A Q 5

♣ 6 4 3

If West gains the lead in the middle of the hand he can lead the ten of clubs. Even if East only has the queen and not both the ace and queen, he is helping to set up a trick in the suit. But in general, be careful to lead through short strong holdings, not long ones, which would be helping declarer to set up tricks.

As with all bridge adages, consider the hand as a whole before making the play. There may be a good reason for doing something else.

Cover an Honour with an Honour

If an *unsupported* honour is led from the dummy, it is usually right to cover it if you are sitting East with a higher honour. Here is a simple example:

♠ J 7

♠ 10 8 4   ♠ K 6 5

♠ A Q 9 3 2

If the jack is led from the dummy and East does not cover with the king, the jack will be run (finessed). Then the declarer will play another

spade to his queen and pick up the suit for no losers. But what happens
when East covers the jack with the king? South can win with the ace
and cash the queen, but then West's ten will be high. Of course East
cannot be sure that his partner has the ten, but it cannot cost to cover
the jack. The position would be the same if the dummy had the queen
and declarer the jack.

However, if the honour that is led is the top of two touching cards,
do *not* cover the first one, cover the *second* one. (These plays are
identical if the declarer leads the honour from his hand, but as this is
hidden it might be difficult for West to decide if the declarer has just
led an unsupported honour or one from two touching honours – these
problems are sent to try you!) Suppose the suit lay-out is like this:

♡ Q J 9

♡ 10 5 3   ♡ K 6 4

♡ A 8 7 2

The queen is led from the dummy; if East covers with the king, South
wins with the ace and then finesses the nine, making four tricks in the
suit. But what happens if East does not cover the queen? Then the
declarer is caught on Morton's Fork.* If he next leads the jack, East
covers with the king (covering the second honour) and the ten is pro-
moted. If instead declarer leads the nine from the dummy, East plays
low and again the defenders are assured of a trick.

If there are three touching honours in the dummy, do not cover any
of them unless you can see that you are setting up a trick for yourself.

◇ Q J 10 8 (dummy)

◇ K 9 6 3 (you)

There is no reason to cover the queen – partner might have the singleton ace! After that you could cover the jack or the ten to make sure
you score a trick with the nine.

◇ Q J 10 8

◇ K 7 6 3

Now there is no advantage in covering any card. You have to hope that
the declarer only has ace-to-three, in which case your king will sit over

---

* John Morton became lord chancellor to Henry VII in 1487 and had a
theory that those with a high cost of living could afford to pay taxes to
the king, while those living frugally were obviously saving money and so
could also afford to pay taxes!

the ten after three rounds of the suit.

This example highlights one important facet of covering an honour with an honour — only do it if you might generate a trick for your side.

$$\clubsuit A J 10 9 8 7$$

$$\clubsuit K 6 4$$

If the declarer leads the queen, what is the point in covering? It cannot gain a trick.

$$\spadesuit J 7 6 5 3$$

$$\spadesuit K 4$$

If South has opened one spade and received support, it cannot gain to cover the jack of spades. At the worst your partner will hold either the singleton ace or the singleton queen!

There is one other position when it is virtually always right to cover an honour with an honour: when you have a doubleton honour and your partner has led the honour below yours. If you play a low card the suit might become blocked.

$$\diamondsuit 8 6 5 3$$

$$\diamondsuit K Q J 9 \qquad \diamondsuit A 2$$

$$\diamondsuit 10 7 4$$

Partner leads the king; you should overtake with the ace and return the two. If you play the two on the first round the suit will be blocked by your ace on the second round.

$$\heartsuit 7 5 4$$

$$\heartsuit Q J 10 8 3 \qquad \heartsuit K 9$$

$$\heartsuit A 6 2$$

Partner leads the queen; put on the king. If you duck the declarer can either take with the ace immediately, blocking the suit, or, if it is a no-trump contract, duck twice, leaving you on play without a third heart to lead.

That covers the key defensive manoeuvres. Try the quiz hands to see if you have grasped the basics. The last problem is more difficult; if you get it right you are well on the way to becoming a good bridge player.

QUIZ

1. Defending against a no-trump contract, you decide to lead from these suits; which are the correct cards to lead?
a. K Q 10 9   b. A J 10 7 6   c. A J 9 4 3 2   d. 10 9 8 6

2. This time you are on lead against a suit contract. You decide to lead this side-suit; which is the correct card to lead in each case?
a. K Q 7 6   b. A 6 4 3   c. A J 10 6   d. 6 4 3

3. Defending against a no-trump contract your partner leads the two of clubs, an unbid suit. The dummy comes down with ♣ J 8 3. The declarer calls for the three; which card do you play from each of these holdings?
a. Q 9 4   b. K Q 4   c. 7 6 5 4   d. 6 5 4

4. Partner leads the king of hearts against four spades, an unbid suit during the auction. Which cards do you play from your holdings when the dummy appears with ♡ J 8 3?
a. 7 5   b. A 4   c. 7 6 4   d. 7 6 4 2

5. What do you understand by the following expressions?
a. The Bath Coup b. A suit preference signal   c. A count signal
d. The Rule of Eleven.

6. South opens one spade and North raises to four spades; which opening leads would you make with these hands?

a. ♠ A 5 4
♡ 6
◇ 10 8 6 4 3
♣ 9 7 6 2

b. ♠ A K Q
♡ 9 7 6 5
◇ 7 5 4
♣ 4 3 2

c. ♠ 7 5 4
♡ K Q J 10
◇ Q 7 5
♣ J 6 2

d. ♠ 7 5 4
♡ 8 6 5
◇ K J 7 5
♣ 10 5 3

7.

Game all; dealer South.

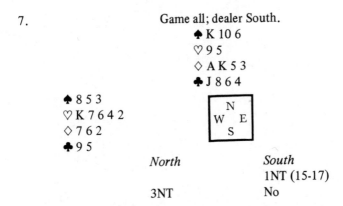

♠ K 10 6
♡ 9 5
◇ A K 5 3
♣ J 8 6 4

♠ 8 5 3
♡ K 7 6 4 2
◇ 7 6 2
♣ 9 5

North	South
	1NT (15-17)
3NT	No

You decide to lead the four of hearts, fourth best. Dummy plays the five, partner wins with the ace and the declarer drops the ten. Your partner returns the eight of hearts and declarer plays the queen; how do you think you can beat the contract?

Answers on page 198

Section C

Rule Number One

— COUNTING —

21   *Keep Counting*

'It's the oldest rule in the book,' said the King.
'Then it ought to be Number One,' said Alice.
Lewis Carroll

Until last I have left in some ways the most important chapter of all.
Success at bridge does involve counting. As I have already said, everyone is capable of it, but it needs conscious effort. You will get as much
out of bridge as you put in; the more you work, concentrate, think,
count at the table, the better the player you will be. And it is not that
difficult. It is just a matter of keeping track of what is going on the
whole time, not wondering what you will be wearing tomorrow, not
thinking about how nice your right-hand opponent looks — leave that
until after the game, or when you have to be the dummy! Keep your
mind on the game. If you set out with that as one of your primary
aims, you will become a good player. How good will depend on how
much of that elusive natural talent called *card sense* you have been
born with, and a little luck. But even if you have no ambition above
being able to play an occasional game, wouldn't you like to make
winning easier?

There were two hands in *Join Us For Bridge* which exhibited the benefits that can be derived from counting.

Game all; dealer West.

♠ A Q 9 2
♡ K J 6 5
◇ 6 5
♣ A J 8

♠ K J 7 4
♡ Q 4 3
◇ 7 4 2
♣ K 7 3

West	North	East	South
1◇	Dble.	No	2♠
No	4♠	No	No
No			

North makes an impeccable take-out double over one diamond, South jumps correctly to two spades, and then North makes an aggressive leap to game. I think three spades would be better, giving partner some leeway, but with his actual hand South would go on to game.

West leads two top diamonds, the ace and king, before switching to a trump. You draw three rounds ending in hand, East throwing a club on the third round. You play a heart to the king, but East wins with the ace and returns the ten. You take this with the queen, the honour in the shorter hand first, and cross to the jack of hearts, but West discards a diamond. What do you do about the club suit? What do you know about the hand?

West opened the bidding and should have thirteen points including distribution. You are only missing sixteen high-card points, and East has produced the ace of hearts. So West must have the queen of clubs to make up an opening bid. Cross to the king of clubs and finesse the jack, expecting the full deal to look like this:

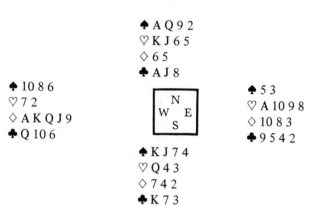

♠ A Q 9 2
♥ K J 6 5
♦ 6 5
♣ A J 8

♠ 10 8 6
♥ 7 2
♦ A K Q J 9
♣ Q 10 6

N
W E
S

♠ 5 3
♥ A 10 9 8
♦ 10 8 3
♣ 9 5 4 2

♠ K J 7 4
♥ Q 4 3
♦ 7 4 2
♣ K 7 3

On that hand counting the points was the most important thing, the bidding giving a guide as to the division of the high-cards among the

— VISUALISING THE OPPONENT'S HAND —

defenders. This hand involves counting the suit distributions.

Game all; dealer South.

♠ K 10 2
♡ A J 8 4
◇ A Q 6 3
♣ Q 7

♠ A J 6 5
♡ K Q 7 5
◇ K 5
♣ K 8 4

North	South
	1NT
2♣	2♡
4NT	5◇
6♡	No

North used Stayman to try to uncover a four-four major-suit fit, and after succeeding in locating one, she used Blackwood. Though she had two club losers, opposite a strong no-trump it was reasonable to expect her partner to have either the ace or the king, especially as she knew they had 31-33 high-card points between them. Over the one ace reply, North settled for six hearts. The opening lead is the eight of diamonds; how would you plan to play the hand? Give it some thought before reading on.

You must lose a trick to the ace of clubs, and you have to find the queen of spades — not the world's best contract! If the trumps are four-one things will become very difficult because there is a diamond to ruff in hand and a club to ruff in the dummy, so you must assume that the hearts will break three-two. The important thing is to leave the key suit, spades, until last; try to find out as much as possible about the other suits first.

Win the diamond lead in hand (the honour in the short hand first) and draw trumps in three rounds, ending in hand; you discover that West has only two as she throws the two of clubs on the third round. Now play a club towards the queen; if West goes in with the ace you will be home without guessing the spade as one of the dummy's spades can be thrown on the king of clubs. But in fact East takes the queen with the ace and plays back the ten of clubs, which you win with the king. This is what you can see at this point:

♠ K 10 2
♡ J
◇ A Q 6
♣ None

♠ A J 6 5
♡ 7
◇ 5
♣ 8

Leave the spades alone until the last moment; ruff a club, everyone follows, and then take the ace of diamonds — ah, West discards the three of spades. What does that tell you? West had a singleton diamond, she also had two hearts, and we have seen four clubs: she followed to all three rounds and she discarded one on the third round of hearts. Now looking at East: we know he had six diamonds and three hearts at the beginning of the hand, and he has followed to all three rounds of clubs; how many spades did he start with? Correct — at most one. His last card could be the thirteenth club, or it could be a spade. So do you see how to guarantee the contract from here? Yes, play a low spade to the ace. In fact East follows with the seven; he was initially 1-3-6-3 shape. Now you play the five of spades and finesse dummy's ten, *knowing* that it will win. You cash the king of spades and the queen of diamonds, throwing your last spade, before cross-ruffing the last two tricks: the six of diamonds is ruffed in hand and the eight of clubs is trumped in the dummy.

It is not too difficult as long as you watch all the cards carefully, remember that every suit has thirteen cards in it, and that every player began with exactly thirteen cards too.

If you think that will be too much for you at the beginning, start by counting the trump suit every time there is one, whether you are the declarer or one of the defenders. That will be an important first step up the road to becoming a good bridge player.

In fact, if you are still reading this book, you have probably been firmly bitten by the bridge bug, and he will be more adhesive than the most persistent limpet or barnacle. Do not fight — submit, try your hardest, and the best of luck!

QUIZ

1. ♠ 7 6 5
    ♡ K 8 7 6
    ◇ K J 10
    ♣ K 4 3

West	North	East	South
			1♡
1♠	3♡	No	4♡
No	No	No	

♠ J 9 2
♡ A Q J 5
◇ A 5 4
♣ A Q 6

West cashes the ace, king and queen of spades, East following once and throwing two clubs, before switching to a trump. You draw three rounds of trumps, West following every time and East parting with a diamond. How do you continue?

2. ♠ A J 9 6
    ♡ J 7 6 5
    ◇ J 5
    ♣ K Q 4

West	North	East	South
			1♡
4◇	4♡	No	No
No			

♠ K 8 4 3
♡ K Q 10 9
◇ 8 6
♣ A 7 6

Being vulnerable South opens one heart, his lower four-card suit, West makes the annoying pre-emptive four diamond overcall and North bids four hearts, which is passed out.

West cashes the ace and king of diamonds, East petering, before switching to the jack of clubs. You win in the dummy and play a low heart, but East whistles in with the ace to return a club. You play low and West discards a diamond; how do you continue?

Answers on page 200

Quiz Answers

This trade of mine — I don't know, can't be sure
But there is something in it, tricks and all!
Really, I want to light up my own mind.
Robert Browning

These are the answers to the quizzes set at the end of each chapter. The numbers in parentheses show where the quizzes can be found.

Chapter 2 (Page 22)
1a. Nine (3 + 6) b. Twelve c. Ten d. Nine.
2. The legal auctions are *a*, *c* and *e*. Sequence *b* is illegal because one cannot overcall one diamond with one club. Auction *d* has not finished because there must be three consecutive passes after any positive bid, which includes double or redouble, to end the bidding. At the point reached South has to make a bid. If he passes that will end the auction, but if he does anything else the bidding must continue until there have been three consecutive passes. Finally, in *f* East made an insufficient bid when he overcalled two hearts with two diamonds; one must bid at least three diamonds to overcall two hearts in diamonds.
3. You can play in four partscore contracts and still not have made game. If you play each time in either one club or one diamond, they score only 20 points below the line, so after four of them you would have 80 below the line, still not the 100 needed to make game. If, of course, you play in and make one of a minor on the fifth hand as well you will have scored the 100 points for game.

Those of you with a particular type of mind will claim that the answer is infinite because if you keep going down in your partscore contracts, you will never make game. That is correct, but I hope you realised what I meant by the question!
4a. 60 below the line b. 60 below the line and 20 above
c. 50 above the line d. 70 below the line and 60 above
e. 120 below the line and 500 above f. 700 above the line

g. 120 below the line, and above the line 50 for the insult, 400 for the overtricks and either 500 for a three game rubber or 700 if it were a two game rubber

h. 400 above the line i. 200 below the line and 50 above

j. 400 below the line and either 2150 or 2350 above the line!

5. The biggest penalty one can concede is 4000 for seven down doubled and redoubled in a vulnerable grand slam.

Chapter 3 (Page 31)

1a. Eighteen in high-cards and one distributional point for the fifth spade: a total of nineteen

b. Six: three for the king, two for the long spades and one for the fifth heart

c. Eighteen, all in high-cards

d. Nineteen, counting the one for the fifth club.

2a. One spade b. No bid c. One heart d. One club e. One club

f. One club g. One spade h. One club.

Chapter 4 (Page 42)

1ai. One no-trump ii. One diamond bi. One heart ii. One heart

ci. One diamond ii. One no-trump di. One no-trump ii. One diamond.

2ai. Two clubs, proposing to rebid three clubs, the weakness take-out into clubs. This hand will almost certainly make more tricks in three clubs than in one no-trump. ii. Two clubs; the same holds true here.

bi. Two spades ii. Three spades; counting the long spade you have ten points, just enough to force to game.

ci. Two clubs, Stayman ii. Two clubs, Stayman

di. Two clubs; you have just enough to risk Stayman in the hope of finding the spade fit. If partner responds two diamonds or two hearts, rebid two no-trumps. ii. Two clubs; now you have enough points for game, but start by looking for the spade fit. If partner responds two of a red suit, rebid three no-trumps.

3a. Four spades; you know your partner has enough to try for game with four spades; as you have a good-looking thirteen points, bid game in spades.

b. No bid; your partner has made a weakness take-out into clubs; you are not allowed to bid again.

c. Four spades; with a maximum and three trumps, bid on to game opposite partner's game-try.

d. Two spades; partner has a weak hand with both majors and you prefer spades to hearts.

e. No bid; partner has signed off.

4a.	*West*	*East*	b.	*West*	*East*	c.	*West*	*East*
	1NT	2♠		1NT	2♠		1NT	3NT
	No			2♡	3NT		No	
				4♠	No			

d.	*West*	*East*	e.	*West*	*East*
	1NT	4♠		1NT	3♠
	No			3NT	4♡
				No	

Chapter 5 (Page 51)

1a. One no-trump b. Three diamonds c. Two spades d. Three no-trumps e. Three diamonds f. Two no-trumps g. Two diamonds h. One spade.

2a. Three hearts b. Two spades c. Two diamonds (or two no-trumps) d. Four hearts e. One no-trump f. Three no-trumps g. Two hearts h. Four hearts.

Chapter 6 (Page 60)

1a. Two hearts; you are not quite worth three hearts.

b. Two hearts c. Four spades; this contract must have some play, but if you are feeling a little pessimistic, make a game-try with three hearts and pass if partner only rebids three spades.

d. Three hearts e. Three hearts f. Four spades g. Four hearts h. No bid.

Chapter 7 (Page 63)

1ai. Four spades ii. Four spades bi. Four spades (or three spades if you are feeling cautious) ii. Two spades; you do not have enough for game opposite 12-14 points, so settle in the safest contract with the known eight- or nine-card fit.

ci. Two no-trumps (or no bid) ii. No bid di. Three hearts ii. Two hearts.

2a. No bid b. Three hearts c. Four spades (or three spades)

d. Two no-trumps (or three no-trumps if feeling particularly aggressive) e. Three clubs f. Two spades (three spades is an overbid after you have already responded at the two level) g. Four spades h. Four hearts; all your high-cards are working and justify bidding game rather than the pusillanimous three hearts.

3a. Three diamonds b. No bid c. Three hearts d. Two no-trumps.

Chapter 8 (Page 70)

1. The reverses are *a*, *c* and *e*, the last being part of the definition of the responder's reverse because the new suit, clubs, is shown at the three level. Auctions *b* and *d* are not reverses because one cannot make a reverse at the one level.

2. Hand *a* is the only one with which it is correct to reverse. Hand *b* does not have enough points and *c* contains only one four-card or longer suit.

3. Hand *b* is just about worth a responder's reverse, and *c* has easily enough points.

4a. *West*	*East*	b. *West*	*East*	c. *West*	*East*
1♠	2◇	1◇	2♣	1◇	2♣
2♠	3♣	2◇	2♡	2◇	2♡
3NT	No	4♡	No	3♣	3NT
				No	

Chapter 9 (Page 72)

1a. One diamond b. One club c. One heart.

2a. Two diamonds; ignore those weak clubs; show where your points lie. b. No bid c. This is a borderline case with four clubs, three clubs and three diamonds all coming in for consideration. Because of the weak clubs, which means that three no-trumps could well be the right contract, I think one should either make the underbid of three clubs or the overbid of three diamonds, depending on how one is feeling at the time. d. Four diamonds e. No bid or three clubs, the latter being a game-try in one's weakest suit; I think three clubs is better than a pass because game could be on.

Chapter 10 (Page 77)

1. Only hand *c* should use fourth suit forcing; *a* bids three no-trumps, *b* should have bid one spade on the first round, not two clubs, and *d* rebids three clubs.

2a. Three clubs b. Two no-trumps c. Three spades d. Three no-trumps e. Two spades f. Three diamonds.

Chapter 11 (Page 88)

1a. Two spades b. Two clubs c. Two clubs d. Two clubs.

2ai. Three spades ii. Two no-trumps iii. Two diamonds

bi. Three hearts; you are too strong for an immediate four hearts.
ii. Three hearts iii. Two hearts
ci. Three clubs, proposing to pass whatever partner bids.
ii. Two no-trumps iii. Two diamonds
di. Three clubs, proposing to bid four clubs on the next round.
This hand is too good to bid only three no-trumps in my opinion.
ii. Three clubs iii. Three clubs.
3a. Three spades b. Three hearts c. Three no-trumps; an unusual hand
because you have nine tricks lay-down in no-trumps as long as they
cannot cash five club tricks, making this contract a good bet.
d. What did you bid? Three spades? I hope you realised that this hand
is not worth a two spade opening bid, making it an impossible question.
Just checking you are still awake!
4a. Four spades, showing the fit and not a complete Yarborough.
b. Three diamonds (or three spades) c. Three spades d. Four clubs.
5ai. Three spades ii. Three no-trumps bi. Two no-trumps ii. No bid
ci. Three diamonds i. Three clubs, Stayman
di. Three hearts ii. Four hearts.

Chapter 12 (Page 93)

1a. Three spades b. No bid; you have a side four-card major.
c. No bid; you do not have enough playing tricks to open three clubs.
d. Three no-trumps.
2a. No bid b. Four hearts; a tactical raise. c. Three spades
d. Six hearts; he must have seven hearts to the ace-queen, giving you a
good play for a slam.
3a. No bid; you have the stoppers. b. Four clubs c. Six clubs; expecting
to lose only to the ace of hearts. d. Four clubs (or five clubs as a tactical bid if non-vulnerable against vulnerable).

Chapter 13 (Page 98)

1. Blackwood has just been bid in auctions *a* and *c*. Four no-trumps is
never Blackwood if the last bid was in no-trumps; and in *d* no suit has
been agreed, so four no-trumps is a sign-off.
2. Cue-bids have just been made in auctions *a*, *c* and *d*. In *a* hearts have
clearly been agreed; but in *c* it is not so obvious. The responder's bid
of three spades showed at least five spades and was forcing to game. So
far I have told you that the opener either bids three no-trumps, with
only two spades, or four spades with three or four cards in spades.
But occasionally the opener will have such a good hand for play in

spades that he wants to suggest a slam in case the responder is interested. He does this by cue-bidding his lowest ace at the four level. If the responder can envisage a slam he can cue-bid in return or use Blackwood, but if he only wants to play in game he signs off with four spades. The opener might hold something like this:

♠ K Q 5 4 ♡ 6 5 ◇ K 5 4 ♣ A Q 8 6. In auction *d* the responder used Stayman, the opener showed four hearts and the responder promised four spades with enough points to have a slam in mind. Given that, if the opener does not have four spades he bids no-trumps, but if he does and he likes his hand, he cue-bids his lowest ace at the four level to give the responder the good news. This time the opener has the ace of diamonds but not the ace of clubs, perhaps

♠ A Q 8 6 ♡ A K 5 4 ◇ A Q 4 ♣ Q 4.

3. Do *not* use Blackwood or Gerber with:

(a) two losers in an unbid suit unless you are certain partner has a control in the suit

(b) a void

(c) do not bid five no-trumps for kings unless you have all the aces.

4. The responder's bid of four hearts has shown the values for a positive response and heart support, but it has denied an ace, so there is little point in four no-trumps asking for aces. In this case four no-trumps asks for *kings*; it is called the Acol Direct King. If you follow up with five no-trumps over your partner's response you are asking for queens and telling him that you have all the aces and all the kings. Well done if you got that one right; if you got all the questions correct in this chapter: fantastic!

Chapter 14 (Page 102)

1a. One no-trump b. No bid c. Two clubs (or two no-trumps or double)
d. Two no-trumps e. Two clubs (or two spades) f. Two diamonds.
2a. No bid; not quite worth a double with only two small hearts and eight points. b. Double c. Two hearts d. Two spades.

Chapter 15 (Page 107)

1ai. No bid ii. One no-trump bi. One heart ii. One heart
ci. Two spades (or one spade) ii. Two spades
di. One spade ii. Two spades (or one spade)
ei. One heart if non-vulnerable, otherwise no bid. ii. One heart (or no bid) fi. One no-trump ii. Double.
2a. One spade b. No bid c. One no-trump d. Three no-trumps

e. Two hearts; the king of diamonds can be devalued, but one might bid three hearts if feeling very aggressive.

f. Three no-trumps g. Two diamonds, followed by a minimum spade bid, which will be forcing as you have started with a cue-bid.

h. Two spades (or two diamonds if feeling optimistic).

3a. Two spades b. Two hearts c. Three no-trumps d. Three spades.

4a. Three no-trumps b. Two diamonds; the cue-bid of their suit acts as Stayman. c. No bid d. Two spades, a weakness take-out.

5a. Three no-trumps b. Three no-trumps; you could bid two hearts, cue-bid Stayman, but the length in hearts suggest that even if your partner has four spades, they might beat four spades by getting in a heart ruff or two. Three no-trumps should be safe.

c. Two no-trumps d. Two spades.

6a. Three hearts, forcing after a jump overcall, remember.

b. Three no-trumps c. No bid; you have no reason to assume that hearts will be better than spades, and you do not have enough points to make a forcing three heart bid. d. Four spades.

Chapter 16 (Page 115)

1. The hands that are strong enough and suitable for a take-out double are *b* and *f*. Hand *a* is not strong enough to double, *c* should overcall one no-trump, *d* bids one heart and *e* bids two diamonds, an immediate cue-bid because you can make game in your own hand.

2a. One no-trump b. Two diamonds c. No bid d. Two no-trumps e. Two clubs f. Two diamonds g. Two diamonds h. Two hearts.

3a. Two hearts; game-forcing one-suiter. b. Two diamonds c. Redouble; looking for a penalty. d. One no-trump e. No bid; there is nothing you can do on this round. f. Redouble g. Three diamonds h. Two no-trumps.

4a. Three spades b. Double c. Three no-trumps; remember that you are assuming partner has seven points. d. No bid; you must hope partner reopens with a double in the protective position, which you will pass, converting it to a penalty double.

5a. Three spades b. Four hearts c. Three no-trumps d. No bid; go for penalty.

Chapter 17 (Page 131)

1a. Six b. None c. Three d. Four.

2a. Four winners and no losers b. Two tricks and one loser

c. One winner and three losers d. Probably one winner and two losers, but if you can find an opponent with ace-doubleton you can make two tricks and restrict yourself to one loser.

3a. Lead towards either the king or queen, let us say the queen. If East plays low, put up the queen. Whether it wins or loses, finesse the nine on the second round if West plays low.

b. Lead the jack and run it if West plays low. It will have to win if you are to make three tricks, and then you finesse the queen on the second round. Note that it is better to run the jack than to play low to the queen or ten. In this second case the lead will be in the dummy (North) and you will have to get back to hand to repeat the finesse. If you run the jack on the first round you stay in the South hand and can repeat the finesse immediately.

c. Finesse the nine on the first round, and finesse the queen on the second if the nine loses to the ten or jack and West does not produce the king on the second round when you lead towards the North hand.

d. This is a tough one because it depends upon the opponents. The correct start is to lead low to the king. If East is a player who will always win this trick with the ace if he has it, and the king holds the trick, return to the South hand, lead another round of the suit and put up the queen if West plays low. However, if East is a player who will let the king win on the first round even if he has the ace (which is normally the correct play), return to the South hand and run the ten.

If the king is taken by the ace on the first round, get back to the South hand and run the ten, finessing West for the jack.

4a. The maximum is three (West has both the king and jack) and the minimum is one (East has the two missing honours).

b. The maximum is three (West has specifically A Q x) and the minimum one (East has the ace-queen doubleton or ace-queen-to-four or more).

c. The maximum is five (the suit divides three-three or either opponent has the jack-ten doubleton) and the minimum is three (East has at least five cards headed by the jack or ten).

d. The maximum is five, West having the queen, the ace or both honours, and the minimum is four, East having both the ace and queen.

Chapter 18 (Page 143)

1a. The correct play is to win the heart lead in hand with either the king or jack, depending on the card played by East, and then to lead a club. You will be able to knock out the ace and king of clubs and end with two spade, three heart, two diamond and two club tricks. Taking a finesse in spades or diamonds could lead to defeat if the full deal is like this:

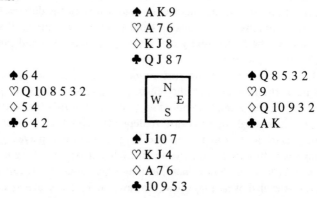

```
                      ♠ A K 9
                      ♡ A 7 6
                      ◇ K J 8
                      ♣ Q J 8 7
   ♠ 6 4                                    ♠ Q 8 5 3 2
   ♡ Q 10 8 5 3 2         N                 ♡ 9
   ◇ 5 4                W     E              ◇ Q 10 9 3 2
   ♣ 6 4 2                  S                ♣ A K
                      ♠ J 10 7
                      ♡ K J 4
                      ◇ A 7 6
                      ♣ 10 9 5 3
```

Whichever losing finesse you take at trick two, East can return that suit and you will lose five tricks before making nine.

b. You have eight top tricks, so you need to find one more to make three no-trumps. You can hope that either diamonds or clubs break three-three, but the advantage of trying the clubs is that you need only lose the lead once, whereas in diamonds you will have to play low twice (to play off the ace and another risks the opposition cashing four tricks in the suit if it breaks five-one). The best play is to win the heart lead with the ace or king and then duck a club in both hands. If the opposition continues hearts, take it and play off the king of clubs (the honour from the short hand first) and the ace of clubs. If the suit breaks three-three you are home; if not you need a miracle: diamonds three-three with East having the king-queen-jack and hearts five-two.

This is a possible full deal:

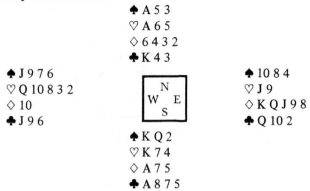

```
                    ♠ A 5 3
                    ♡ A 6 5
                    ◇ 6 4 3 2
                    ♣ K 4 3
    ♠ J 9 7 6                        ♠ 10 8 4
    ♡ Q 10 8 3 2      N              ♡ J 9
    ◇ 10          W       E          ◇ K Q J 9 8
    ♣ J 9 6           S              ♣ Q 10 2
                    ♠ K Q 2
                    ♡ K 7 4
                    ◇ A 7 5
                    ♣ A 8 7 5
```

c. The correct play is to put up dummy's queen of hearts at trick one and see what happens. If it wins you know that West has the ace and so you must keep East off the lead, otherwise he can play a heart through your king and you could lose one diamond and four heart tricks. The right play, if dummy's queen of hearts wins the first trick, is to cash the ace of diamonds and then to finesse the jack if East produces a small card for the second time. Even if it loses you have nine tricks.

However, if East wins the queen of hearts with the ace and returns a heart, duck it and win the third round of the suit. Then cash the *king* of diamonds and finesse the ten if West plays two low cards. If East wins with the queen and has a heart to play the suit must have broken four-four and you will only lose one diamond and three heart tricks.

This hand highlights the danger of following too closely sayings like 'eight ever, nine never'. Depending on the play at the first trick, even though you have nine diamonds, it is correct to take a finesse on the second round.

The full deal might be:

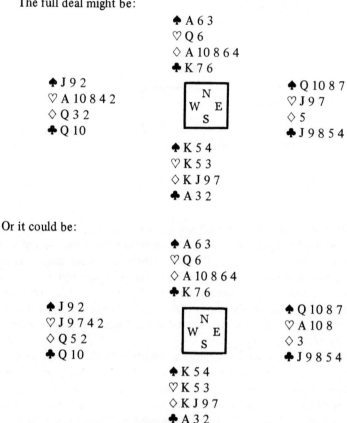

```
                    ♠ A 6 3
                    ♡ Q 6
                    ◇ A 10 8 6 4
                    ♣ K 7 6
♠ J 9 2                                ♠ Q 10 8 7
♡ A 10 8 4 2          N                ♡ J 9 7
◇ Q 3 2          W         E           ◇ 5
♣ Q 10               S                 ♣ J 9 8 5 4
                    ♠ K 5 4
                    ♡ K 5 3
                    ◇ K J 9 7
                    ♣ A 3 2
```

Or it could be:

```
                    ♠ A 6 3
                    ♡ Q 6
                    ◇ A 10 8 6 4
                    ♣ K 7 6
♠ J 9 2                                ♠ Q 10 8 7
♡ J 9 7 4 2          N                 ♡ A 10 8
◇ Q 5 2          W         E           ◇ 3
♣ Q 10               S                 ♣ J 9 8 5 4
                    ♠ K 5 4
                    ♡ K 5 3
                    ◇ K J 9 7
                    ♣ A 3 2
```

d. This hand is similar to the last except that you should duck two rounds of hearts, winning the third. It is then comparable with the case when the queen of hearts lost to the ace in the above hand. You should cash the king of diamonds, proposing to finesse the ten on the second round if West plays two small diamonds. This is the deal you must cater for:

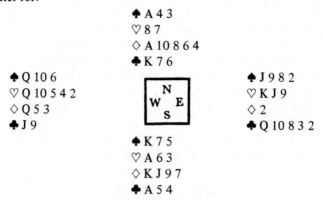

```
                    ♠ A 4 3
                    ♡ 8 7
                    ◇ A 10 8 6 4
                    ♣ K 7 6
  ♠ Q 10 6                              ♠ J 9 8 2
  ♡ Q 10 5 4 2        N                 ♡ K J 9
  ◇ Q 5 3          W     E              ◇ 2
  ♣ J 9               S                 ♣ Q 10 8 3 2
                    ♠ K 7 5
                    ♡ A 6 3
                    ◇ K J 9 7
                    ♣ A 5 4
```

If you have found any of these hands hard to visualise, get out a pack of cards and play them through for yourself, trying the different possible distributions of the East-West cards. You will find that the recommended plays win more often than any others.

Chapter 19 (Page 149)

1a. This is a tricky hand; did you finesse the diamond at trick one? If you did, you will go down against best defence if the full deal is like this:

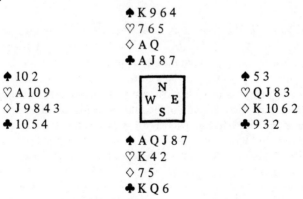

```
                    ♠ K 9 6 4
                    ♡ 7 6 5
                    ◇ A Q
                    ♣ A J 8 7
  ♠ 10 2                               ♠ 5 3
  ♡ A 10 9            N                ♡ Q J 8 3
  ◇ J 9 8 4 3      W     E             ◇ K 10 6 2
  ♣ 10 5 4            S                ♣ 9 3 2
                    ♠ A Q J 8 7
                    ♡ K 4 2
                    ◇ 7 5
                    ♣ K Q 6
```

If you finesse in diamonds at trick one East will win and return the queen of hearts, allowing the defenders to take one diamond and three heart tricks.

The correct play is to rise with the ace of diamonds at trick one, draw trumps and run the clubs, giving you five spade, one diamond and four club tricks for your contract. (In fact on the last club you can pitch the seven of diamonds and lead a heart towards your king to try for an overtrick without endangering your contract.)

b. You have nine top tricks: five spades, one heart and three diamonds after the lead. The best play for the tenth trick is to ruff a heart in the dummy. So win the opening trick in hand with either the king or jack of diamonds, depending on the card the East plays, and play the ace of hearts and a small heart. You will be able to gain access to the South hand in the trump suit, ruff a heart with the *jack* of spades and draw trumps to claim ten tricks. This might be the full deal:

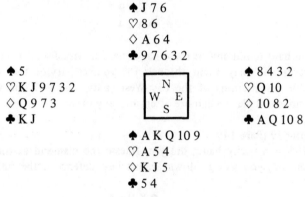

```
              ♠ J 7 6
              ♡ 8 6
              ◇ A 6 4
              ♣ 9 7 6 3 2
 ♠ 5                              ♠ 8 4 3 2
 ♡ K J 9 7 3 2      N             ♡ Q 10
 ◇ Q 9 7 3      W       E         ◇ 10 8 2
 ♣ K J              S             ♣ A Q 10 8
              ♠ A K Q 10 9
              ♡ A 5 4
              ◇ K J 5
              ♣ 5 4
```

c. If you win the first trick with the ace of diamonds and play a trump, the defence will probably be able to take four tricks: the ace of spades, the king of diamonds and the ace-king of clubs. To stop this you must delay playing trumps until after you have discarded a loser on the third round of hearts. So rise with the ace of diamonds at trick one and play three rounds of hearts, throwing the nine of diamonds (or a club). If that has passed off safely, play a spade to dislodge the ace.

The full deal:

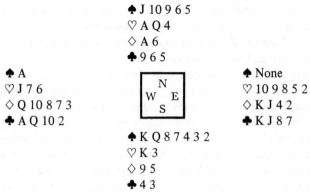

♠ J 10 9 6 5
♡ A Q 4
◇ A 6
♣ 9 6 5

♠ A
♡ J 7 6
◇ Q 10 8 7 3
♣ A Q 10 2

N
W E
S

♠ None
♡ 10 9 8 5 2
◇ K J 4 2
♣ K J 8 7

♠ K Q 8 7 4 3 2
♡ K 3
◇ 9 5
♣ 4 3

d. On this hand the playing of trumps must be postponed as well. If you win the first trick with the ace of diamonds and play a spade, the defence can win with the ace, cash a diamond trick and switch to hearts. When they get in with the ace of clubs they will cash a heart trick to bring their total to four. The way to stop this treachery is to win with the ace of diamonds and play a club. Let us assume that they take this with the ace, cash a top diamond and switch to hearts. You win with the ace and cash the king of clubs, throwing your heart loser from the South hand. Only then is it safe to play spades.

The full deal:

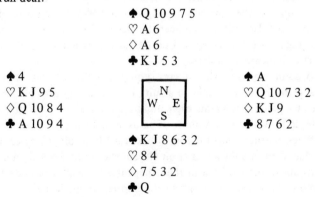

♠ Q 10 9 7 5
♡ A 6
◇ A 6
♣ K J 5 3

♠ 4
♡ K J 9 5
◇ Q 10 8 4
♣ A 10 9 4

N
W E
S

♠ A
♡ Q 10 7 3 2
◇ K J 9
♣ 8 7 6 2

♠ K J 8 6 3 2
♡ 8 4
◇ 7 5 3 2
♣ Q

Chapter 20 (Page 172)

1a. The king, the top of touching honours. b. The jack c. The four, fourth highest. d. The ten, the top of a sequence.

2a. The king b. The ace; never underlead an ace against a suit contract. c. The ace d. The four, starting MUD.

3a. The nine, finessing against the dummy. b. The queen, the bottom of touching honours when following suit. c. The five, preparing to play the four next to show an even number. d. The four.

4a. The seven, starting a peter with a doubleton. b. The ace, proposing to return the four, hoping for a ruff at trick three. (However, if you think the declarer could well hold only two, play the four, happy to take two tricks without setting up a winner for the declarer.)

c. The four, low from three and discouraging at the same time. d. The two, discouraging. If you start a peter partner might think you hold only two and try to give you a ruff with potentially fatal consequences to the defence.

5a. The Bath Coup occurs when a suit is distributed like this:

```
                    8 6 4
     K Q 10 9                    7 3 2
                    A J 5
```

On the lead of the king, South plays the *five*, hoping West will continue the suit and give him two tricks in it.

b. A suit preference signal occurs when one partner gives the other a ruff. Suppose the contract is in spades and West is about to give East a heart ruff. He leads a high heart to suggest that East return a diamond (the higher of the other two suits) after getting his ruff, or a low heart to indicate a club return.

c. A count signal is what it says: you give a signal to tell your partner how many cards you hold in a suit. To play a high card before a lower one, to peter, shows an even number, whereas to play in ascending order indicates an odd number of cards in that suit.

d. When partner leads his fourth best card in a suit, if the actual value of that card is subtracted from eleven, the result gives the number of cards above the card led in the other three hands. So by consulting the dummy, both the declarer and the partner of the leader can calculate how many cards above the one led the other holds.

6a. The six of hearts; with trump control, the ace of spades, hope that you can get your partner in to give you a heart ruff.

b. The queen (or ace) of spades; it is best to look at the dummy, and when the queen holds your partner will probably guess you have the ace and king. In the trump suit only you can sometimes break the normal leading rules.

c. The king of hearts; a safe sequence that could set up a trick or two for the defence.

d. The five of diamonds; the opposition sound confident, so try an attacking lead. Second choice: a trump.

7. From the play of the heart suit it is obvious that declarer started with ♡ Q J 10 and your partner with ♡ A 8 3. But if you win the second trick with the king of hearts and clear the suit by playing a third round, how will you get in to cash your last two heart winners? The answer is to play *low* at trick two. It is likely that partner will regain the lead before declarer has wrapped up nine tricks, he will lead his third heart and you can cash three tricks in the suit to beat the contract. This could be the full deal:

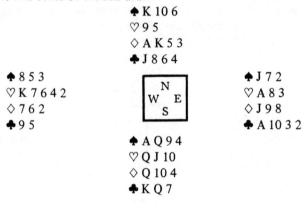

```
                    ♠ K 10 6
                    ♡ 9 5
                    ◇ A K 5 3
                    ♣ J 8 6 4
    ♠ 8 5 3            N            ♠ J 7 2
    ♡ K 7 6 4 2    W     E          ♡ A 8 3
    ◇ 7 6 2            S            ◇ J 9 8
    ♣ 9 5                           ♣ A 10 3 2
                    ♠ A Q 9 4
                    ♡ Q J 10
                    ◇ Q 10 4
                    ♣ K Q 7
```

Chapter 21 (Page 182)

1. You know that West began with six spades and three hearts, leaving him with four cards in the minors. You need to find the queen of diamonds to make your contract, and so leave the critical suit until last. After drawing trumps, cash three rounds of clubs. Suppose that West follows to every round, then you know he has at most one diamond. If that is the case, cash the king of diamonds and look closely at West's card. If it is not the queen, run the jack of diamonds confident that it must hold the trick.

If West only follows to two rounds of clubs, you know he began with two diamonds and East with five. This makes it more likely that East has the queen, so cash the king and take the finesse.

If West follows to only one round of clubs, you know that he has three diamonds to East's four. Again the odds favour finessing through East, but only just.

Finally, if West has no clubs, he has four diamonds, so finesse him for the queen of diamonds: cash the ace first and play low to the jack.

This is a possible full deal:

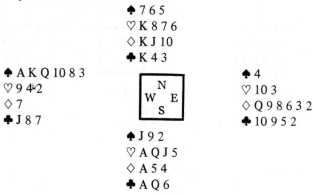

```
                    ♠ 7 6 5
                    ♡ K 8 7 6
                    ◇ K J 10
                    ♣ K 4 3
  ♠ A K Q 10 8 3              ♠ 4
  ♡ 9 4 2              N      ♡ 10 3
  ◇ 7             W       E   ◇ Q 9 8 6 3 2
  ♣ J 8 7              S      ♣ 10 9 5 2
                    ♠ J 9 2
                    ♡ A Q J 5
                    ◇ A 5 4
                    ♣ A Q 6
```

A note in passing: it is very unlikely that West began with a diamond void, because if he did he should cash only the ace and king of spades before leading the *ten* of spades, giving his partner a spade ruff and at the same time giving a suit preference signal for diamonds.

2. You have found out that West began with seven diamonds, one club and presumably only one heart as he did not ruff the second round of clubs. How many spades does that give him? Yes, exactly four. So the correct play is to win the club return in the dummy, you need the ace as a hand entry, draw the trumps and play the king of spades. If East

contributes the queen, play a spade to the nine and claim. If he drops the ten or a low card, play a spade to the nine, return to the ace of clubs and repeat the finesse, again making ten tricks.

This might be the full deal:

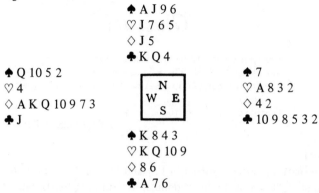

No, I do not approve of West's four diamond bid with four spades in his hand (not to mention the solid diamonds that could make three no-trumps the best contract), but believe the truth of the cards actually played. Just watch closely, saying each card to yourself as it is played (that is my patented method for remembering all the cards; if you do it for every trick you will never miss a card because you have to look at it in order to call it to yourself), and keeping count of the key suit or suits.

Glossary

The first wrote, Wine is the strongest.
The second wrote, The king is strongest.
The third wrote, Women are strongest: but above all
    things
Truth beareth away the victory.

Apocrypha: 1 Esdras

Acol
The natural system devised in England in a bridge club in Acol Road, London. It is still the most popular system in Great Britain and is the basis of this book.

Acol Two Bid
A cornerstone of the Acol system. An opening bid of two spades, hearts or diamonds shows at least eight playing tricks, at least five, and usually six, cards in the bid suit and is forcing for one round.

Auction
Another word for the bidding.

Balanced Hand
A hand with no singleton or void and at most one doubleton
i.e. 4-3-3-3, 4-4-3-2 or 5-3-3-2 shape.

Bath Coup
A play discovered in the city of Bath during the days of whist. This is the standard situation:

```
                    x x x
    K Q x x                      10 9 x
                    A J x
```

When the king is led, South plays low from the A J x. If West continues the suit the declarer, South, gets two tricks in the suit, which he would not if he took the king with the ace and East was able to get the lead to play the ten through the declarer's J x.

Bidding
The initial skilful stage of bridge that occurs after the shuffle and deal. It is like an auction, the two pairs trying to outbid each other to determine who will play the final contract, which suit will be trumps, and how many tricks will have to be made to fulfil the contract.

Blackwood
A convention used to aid slam bidding. When a suit has been agreed, a bid of four no-trumps asks for aces. After receiving the reply on a sliding scale, a bid of five no-trumps asks for kings. The convention should be used primarily to avoid slams that will go down due to a paucity of aces.

Card-Play
The second skilful stage of bridge, occurring after the bidding has been completed.

Card Sense
The elusive quality that all top bridge players are blessed with.

Communications
During the play of the hand, ensuring that it is possible to transfer the lead from the declarer's hand to the dummy or vice versa, or between the defenders' hands, is known as keeping open communications. It is an important aspect of card-play.

Contract
The last bid made in an auction is called the final contract. The bidding side have contracted to make the stated number of tricks in the designated trump suit or no-trumps.

Conventional Bid
A bid, usually in a suit, that has an unnatural meaning, normally bearing no relevance to the suit actually bid. The simplest example is Stayman, when a bid of two clubs over an opening one no-trump asks the opener to show four-card majors; two clubs could be bid with any number of clubs.

Count Signal

During the play of the hand a defender can tell his partner how many cards he has in a suit. He does it by playing a higher card before a lower one, a peter, to show an even number of cards in the suit, or he plays in ascending order to indicate an odd number.

Cross-Ruff

A play that occurs in a suit contract. If the two hands of a partnership have voids in different side-suits they can play each other's void suits and obtain a series of tricks by ruffing.

Cue-Bid

When a suit has been agreed, a bid in another suit at the four level or higher shows a control in that suit, either the ace or a void, or the king or a singleton.

At a lower level a cue-bid is a bid in a suit bid by an opponent. It does not promise a control in the suit, but usually shows a strong hand.

Deal

The distribution of the 52 cards in a clockwise direction, one card to each player in turn, starting with the player on the dealer's left.

Dealer

The person who deals the cards, and who gets the first bid in the auction.

Declarer

The person who will play the cards for the partnership that made the final suit or no-trump bid in the auction.

Defender

One of the players who will try to defeat the declarer in his contract.

Discard

To fail to follow suit, playing a card from a different, non-trump suit to the one led.

Distributional Points

The extra values that you add to the high-card points that take into account the value of long suits, and shortages when a trump fit has been found.

Double Finesse
When the declarer takes two finesses with a given holding in a suit. For example, with A Q 10 opposite small cards, the declarer leads first to the ten, and if that wins or loses to the jack, later plays low to the queen.

Doubleton
A holding of two cards in a suit.

Ducking Play
When a defender or the declarer allows the opposition to win a trick that he could have taken.

Dummy
The partner of the declarer, who puts his cards on the table after the opening lead and takes no further constructive part in the game until the next hand.

Echo
Another word for a peter, a high-low signal to show an even number of cards or to encourage in a suit.

Encouraging/Discouraging Signal
A low card can be used to tell partner that you do not think he has made a good lead or that you do not want a particular suit led (a discouraging signal), whereas the play of a higher card than necessary carries the opposite meaning (an encouraging signal).

Entry
A card with which a player is certain to win a trick during the play of the hand.

Finesse
The play of a lower honour from an honour combination in the hope that a higher honour will be well placed. For example, when holding the ace-queen in a suit in the dummy, lead a low one to the queen in the hope that the king is on the left, permitting two tricks to be won.

Forcing Bid
Any bid that partner is not allowed to pass, such as an Acol Two Bid or Stayman.

Forcing to Game
Any bid or auction which indicates that the bidding must continue until game is reached. For example, a jump shift in response to partner's opening bid.

Fourth Suit Forcing
A bid of the fourth suit in an uncontested auction which indicates that the responder has enough points to consider game a possibility but that he has no convenient bid available. The opener is being asked to describe his hand further.

Game
Obtained when 100 points are scored below the line, either in one go or by adding partscores together.

Game-Forcing
The same as forcing to game.

Game-Try
A bid of a suit, usually asking for help in that suit, as an effort to reach a game contract.

Gerber
A slam convention similar to Blackwood, but used when the last bid was in no-trumps. A bid of four clubs asks for aces, and a subsequent bid of five clubs asks for kings.

Go Down
To fail to fulfil the bid contract.

Grand Slam
A seven-level contract, attempting to take all thirteen tricks.

Hand Diagram
The method by which full deals, or parts of them, are shown in books, magazines and newspaper articles. They save a lot of space over describing everything in words.

High-Card Points
The simplest method by which the strength of a hand is determined. An ace counts as four points, a king three, a queen two and a jack one.

Hold-Up Play
The same as a ducking play.

Honour
An ace, king, queen, jack or ten.

Honour Combination
When holding at least two honours in the same suit.

Honour Points
The same as high-card points.

Jump Overcall
A bid made at least one level higher than was necessary to overcall the preceding bid. For example, two spades over one heart.

Jump Rebid
The second bid by the opener or responder which is one level higher than necessary. For example, after opening one heart and hearing your partner respond one spade, a rebid of three clubs.

Jump Shift
In response to your partner's opening bid, a jump response which shows at least enough points for game. It is an American expression that has entered British bridge vocabulary.

Lavinthal
The name of the American who invented the suit preference signal.

Limit Bid
A bid that defines a player's hand within a close range. For example, a weak no-trump showing 12-14 points, or a single or double raise of partner's one-level opening bid.

Major-Suits
Spades and hearts.

McKenney
The name more commonly given to the suit preference signal because it was McKenney who popularised the defensive technique.

Minor-Suits
Clubs and diamonds.

MUD
An acronym for Middle-Up-Down, the normal sequence adopted in Britain for showing three small cards in a suit when the player decides to lead that suit.

Negative Response
A bid by the responder over an Acol Two Bid to denote a hand too weak to make a positive response. The bids are two diamonds over a a two club opener and, usually, two no-trumps over the other two-level openers.

Non-Forcing
Any bid which may be passed. Of course, that does not mean it must be passed. If the opposite hand has extra values it can bid on. Only if partner makes a sign-off must you pass.

Non-Vulnerable
When a partnership has not yet made a game it is said to be non-vulnerable.

Opener
The person to make the first positive bid in an auction.

Opening Bid
The first positive (i.e. excluding passes) bid made in an auction.

Opening Lead
The first card played to the first trick is the opening lead. It is made by the player to the left of the declarer. After the opening lead the dummy is put down for all to see.

Overcall
When one side has opened the bidding, if an opponent makes a bid in a suit or no-trumps he is said to have made an overcall.

Overtrick
If more tricks are made in the play than were contracted for in the bidding, the extra tricks made are called overtricks. For example, if ten tricks are made in a contract of two clubs there are two overtricks, eight tricks only being needed to fulfil a contract of two clubs.

Partnership
Bridge is played between partnerships with two players in each partnership. They are usually designated by the four cardinal points, North partnering South and East partnering West.

Partscore
Any contract that scores less than 100 points if made is called a partscore.

Penalty Double
A double made when expecting the opponents to go down in their contract. It will increase the points received if they do fail to make their contract, but they will score more if they make it.

Peter
The word given to a high-low signal, playing a high card before a lower one in a suit. Usually it is used to show either an even number of cards in the suit, or to encourage in the suit. Echo is a less commonly used word with the same meaning.

Playing Tricks
The tricks one would expect to make with a given hand excluding the dummy are called the playing tricks. If a hand contains at least eight playing tricks it will normally be worth an Acol Two Bid.

Pre-Emptive Bid
This is a weak bid showing a hand with a long suit, several playing tricks but not many high-card points. Opening bids at the three level or higher, or double jump overcalls are normally pre-emptive bids.

Prepared Club

When using a strong no-trump one occasionally has to open the bidding with a three-card club suit when holding a hand that would have opened a weak no-trump and has 4-3-3-3 or 3-4-3-3 shape. If one opened the hand in the four-card major one would have no rebid available over a two-level response because two no-trumps promises 15-17 points. When opening in a three-card club suit one is said to have begun the auction with a prepared club.

Protective Position

If the opening bid is passed round to you in the fourth position, you are said to be in the protective position because you can bid with slightly less than the usual values to protect partner's known values. (The opener could not bid at the two level, the responder must have less than six points and if you do not have many points, you know your partner must have a reasonable number of high-card values.)

Responder

The partner of the opener.

Responder's Reverse

When the responder bids two suits in ascending order (the second suit is higher-ranking than the first) he is said to have made a reverse unless the auction has gone specifically 1♣-1♢-1♡-1♠. This means that the opener will have to bid at the three level to give preference to the responder's first suit. Because of this fact it is reasonable to expand the definition of a responder's reverse to include the auctions when the responder bids his second suit at the three level, even if it is in a lower-ranking suit. So an auction like 1♡-2♣-2♡-2♠ is a classic responder's reverse, and a sequence like 1♠-2♢-2♠-3♣ fits the expanded definition.

Reverse

A reverse can occur at the two or three level, and happens when either the opener or the responder (see above) bids one suit on the first round and then a new, higher-ranking suit on the second round at a different level. So to open with one heart and rebid two spades on the next round is a reverse because the two suits have been bid at different levels and in ascending order, whereas to open one spade and rebid two hearts is not a reverse. One can tell a reverse that satisfies this definition because the partner of the reverser has to go up to the next level to give preference to the first-bid suit.

Revoke
If one fails to follow suit when one has a card in the suit led, one is said to have revoked.

Rubber
What each partnership tries to win in rubber bridge. The first side to score two games wins the rubber.

Rubber Bridge
The form of bridge in which two partnerships battle against each other, often with a financial involvement, to try to be the first to win two games and in the process hopefully scoring more points than the opposition. The method of scoring is explained in Chapter 2 of this book.

Ruff
When unable to follow suit you can play a trump to try to win a trick — you ruff the trick.

Ruffing Finesse
Suppose that the dummy has the ace-queen-jack of a side-suit in a suit contract and declarer has a singleton with at least one trump. In an effort to score two tricks in the suit he could take a simple finesse by leading low to the queen; but he could also cash the ace and then lead the queen, discarding a loser if it is not covered by the king or ruffing if the king appears, which would set up the jack for a discard later. This is called taking a ruffing finesse.

Rule of Eleven
When the opening leader starts with his fourth highest in a suit, if the value of that spot card is deducted from eleven, the result gives the number of cards above the one led in the other three hands.

Rule of Two and Three
This is the rule that should be borne in mind when making a pre-emptive bid. If both sides are either non-vulnerable or vulnerable, the bidder should anticipate going no more than two down if doubled and the dummy produces no tricks. This means that the penalty will be less than the value of the game the opposition can presumably make, the pre-emptor and his partner both having weak hands in terms of high-

cards. When non-vulnerable against vulnerable opponents one can afford to go three down and still show a profit. (It is not advisable to pre-empt when vulnerable against non-vulnerable.)

Sacrifice
A bid made when one has no expectation of making the contract. The hope is that the penalty will be less than the value of the opponents' contract, thus showing a profit.

Shuffle
The mixing of the cards prior to the deal. The best way to do it is to give the pack six riffle-shuffles.

Signals
Legal manoeuvres by the defenders to give each other information about the number of cards held in the four suits and the location of honour-cards.

Sign-Off
A bid that tells partner he should pass whatever his hand; you are sure that you have just bid the best contract.

Singleton
A holding of only one card in a suit.

Small Slam
A six-level contract, attempting to win twelve tricks.

Stayman
A bid of two clubs over an opening one no-trump bid, or three clubs over a two no-trump opener, asking the opener to show any four-card majors that he holds. It is used to uncover four-four major-suit fits.

Stopper
A holding in a suit that will usually take a trick in a no-trump contract.

Strong No-Trump
An opening bid of one no-trump showing a balanced hand with either 15-17 or 16-18 high-card points.

Suit
One of the four 'families' in a pack of cards: clubs, diamonds, hearts or spades.

Suit-Establishment
A play designed to set up a winner or winners in a suit.

Suit Fit
This tells how many cards a partnership has in any given suit in the two hands. For example, a spade fit of eight cards means that the combined holding in spades is eight when counting both of the partnership's hands.

Suit Preference Signal
When giving your partner a ruff, you will sometimes be able to give him a second ruff if you have an entry in one of the other suits. To tell him which suit you would like him to return after taking his ruff, you give him a suit preference signal. These are also called Lavinthal or McKenney signals.

Take-Out Double
A double that is not intended to be for penalties; quite the opposite: it is asking partner to bid his longest suit, excluding the one bid by the opposition.

Tenace
A holding in a suit where you have a potential 'pincer' position over a card. For example, if North has the ace and queen in a suit and West has the king, that king is held in a pincer between the ace and queen. One normally takes a finesse when holding a tenace.

Trick
Four cards, one from each player, make up a trick. There are thirteen tricks to be won in each hand.

Trump
If the hand is not going to be played in no-trumps, there is a 'master' suit called the trump suit. A trump beats any card from any of the other three suits.

Two-Way Finesse
A finessing position in which you can play either opponent for the critical card. For example, if North has ♡A J 7 and South has ♡K 10 6, one can try for three tricks in the suit by playing either East or West for the queen of hearts.

Unlimited Bid
Any bid for which the upper strength in terms of high-cards is only defined by virtue of the total number of points in the pack. The partner of the player who has made the unlimited bid is not allowed to pass. For example, the responder makes a jump shift response to an opening bid, or the opener starts with an Acol Two Bid.

Variable No-Trump
When playing the variable no-trump one opens with a weak no-trump when non-vulnerable and a strong no-trump when vulnerable.

Void
When holding no cards in a suit one is said to be void of that suit.

Vulnerable
One is said to have become vulnerable after winning a game in rubber bridge.

Weakness Take-Out
This usually occurs over a one no-trump opening bid. When the responder feels that a suit contract will be preferable to playing in one no-trump, he bids two of his suit as a sign-off. (Or he bids two clubs, Stayman, followed by three clubs over the reply if wishing to make a weakness take-out into clubs.) The opener is expected to pass the responder's bid; he has described his hand within fairly close boundaries by his opening bid, so the responder should be able to judge the situation accurately.

Weak No-Trump
An opening bid of one no-trump to show a balanced hand with 12-14 high-card points.